To

Grant,

Thought you might approve
of this! Merry Christmas!

Love
Jackie

RESCUING
THE
SPECTACLED
BEAR

RESCUING THE SPECTACLED BEAR

First published in 2002 by Hutchinson

1 3 5 7 9 10 8 6 4 2

Hutchinson
The Random House Group Limited
20 Vauxhall Bridge Road, London SW1V 2SA

Random House Australia (Pty) Limited
20 Alfred Street, Milsons Point, Sydney
New South Wales 2061, Australia

Random House New Zealand Limited
18 Poland Road, Glenfield
Auckland 10, New Zealand

Random House (Pty) Limited
Endulini, 5a Jubilee Road
Parktown 2193, South Africa

The Random House Group Limited Reg. No. 954009

www.randomhouse.co.uk

A CIP catalogue record for this book is available
from the British Library

Papers used by Random House are natural, recyclable
products made from wood grown in sustainable forests.
The manufacturing processes conform to the
environmental regulations of the country of origin

Designed and typeset by Push, London
Printed and bound by Mohndruck, Gütersloh, Germany

ISBN 0 09 179523 0

A Peruvian Diary

Stephen Fry
With photos by Rob Fraser

HUTCHINSON
LONDON

1

'I had no idea that there were bears in South America.'

'Oh, yes. Yes indeed. Good heavens, yes. Bears in South America? But of course there are. Spectacled Bears. Hundreds of them.'

Welcome

How I was dealt a low blow and came to be interested in Spectacled Bears. The making of Paddington Bear: The Early Years. *The BBC. Will Power versus AC Power.*

'I had no idea that there were bears in South America.'

'Oh, yes. Yes indeed. Good heavens, yes. Bears in South America? But of course there are. Spectacled Bears. Hundreds of them.'

I got very used to this kind of dialogue as I prepared for my first trip to Peru. It was perhaps a little unfair of me to sound so assured about the matter because, until I had looked into it myself, I too had been all unconscious of the existence of bears in Peru. Indeed, most *Peruvians* seem to be unaware of bears in their offing. Unlike some animals – butterflies, peacocks and human beings for example – the Spectacled Bear would much rather not be noticed at all.

The fact that there are bears in Peru might be obvious to anyone who has ever read Michael Bond's Paddington books. Paddington goes with Darkest Peru much as Great Uncle Bulgaria goes with Wimbledon Common and Winnie the Pooh goes with the

Hundred Acre Wood. Yet natural human scepticism might still lead a person to doubt the presence of bears in South America. Just because Michael Bond says so, does it mean that it is true? Writers are known for their relaxed relationship with the truth. For all we know, Michael Bond chose Peru because he liked the way it looked on the page.

It was precisely in order to find out about the origins of Paddington Bear that I travelled to Peru for the first time in May 2001. I have never thought of myself as one of nature's most adventurous travellers. I am devoted to my creature comforts. Which is to say, I am devoted to my human comforts. The kinds of comfort that will do for most creatures fall very far short of my requirements indeed. Most creatures can make do, at a push, without room service, a reliable internet connection and enough power to keep a digital camera, an MP3 Player, an electric razor and a sonic toothbrush fully charged at all times. Not I. Why therefore had I agreed to be a part of a film shot in Peru, a country better known for its drug barons and earthquakes than its de luxe hotels and high speed internet service providers?

It is a melancholy truth that most television companies seem unable to go abroad to look at animals, holiday destinations or wilderness habitats without recruiting an actor or a comedian to front the project. It is probably the fault of Michael Palin, whose skill and natural charm assured the great success of his mighty travel-ogues, *Around the World in Eighty Days* and *Pole to Pole*. Ever since that golden age about forty letters have gone out every week from production companies to Amusing Television Personalities suggesting pro-gramme ideas that range from the worthy to the frankly desperate.

'Dear Mr ~~Laurie~~ Fry, How would you like to go round the world in *forty* days? Twice as good as Michael Palin.'

'Dear Programme-Maker, Wouldn't that mean *half* as good?'

'Dear Stephen Rhys Jones, Would you be interested in visiting all the countries in the world that end in a vowel?'

'Dea Productio Co, No I wou no be intere i visiti a the countrie i th wo tha e wi a vowe.'

'Dear Mr Fry, How about a programme that traces the origins of Paddington Bear?'

'Dear Producer, How about a thick ear?'

Well, it didn't quite go like that, but nonetheless I cannot pretend that the idea of a programme on Paddington's Peruvian roots, when the initial proposal hit the doormat, sent me spinning about the room radiant with joy and purpose.

On such occasions one relies on one's agent. Accepting or declining comes down to two issues: availability and instinct. Well, all right, three issues: availability, instinct and money. Oh, very well, four issues: availability, instinct, money and pampering. But the greatest of these, if one's lucky enough to be reasonably well covered in the areas of mortgage and meat in the fridge, is instinct. My agent, a marvellous woman called Lo, has instinct by the bucketful.

'They seem very nice people,' she said of OR Media, the production company who had sent the letter. 'Very enthusiastic.'

It might seem to some, unfamiliar with the ways of the entertainment industry, that niceness and enthusiasm are side-issues. Surely a kick-ass cynicism combined with experience, ambition and a side order of world-weary cool are what we require in the exciting world of television? Well, the longer you live, the more you come to value such simple virtues as niceness and enthusiasm.

Although I can't remember what I was doing in the autumn of 2000, which is when the first overtures were made, I still wasn't entirely won over by my agent's favourable impression. Niceness and enthusiasm may be ... well, nice, but they are not necessarily enough to send a man like me straight to the outdoor shop to stock up on mosquito nets and water purification tablets.

'Lo, I'm glad they're nice,' I said. 'I'm pleased that they are enthusiastic. But South America. Footsteps of Paddington Bear. It's not really very me, is it? Is it? I mean, is it? Or is it? Mm?'

And there I would probably have left it, were it not for

the diabolical cunning of Sam.

A week or so after talking to Lo, a ring at the doorbell heralded the leather-bound, radio-crackling, clip-boarded presence of a motorcycle courier. I signed for a small square box. Inside the box I found a Paddington Bear. Around his neck, as is usual with Paddington Bears, was a label. This label was different. Instead of saying 'Please look after this bear. Thank you', it said, in a firm but somehow anxious hand, 'Dear Mr Fry, Please take me back to Peru. Thank you.'

I don't know. Maybe I was in a vulnerable or senti-mental mood. Maybe I'm a soft touch. For whatever reason, this entreaty was enough to get me round a table with Nick Green, the OR Media producer responsible for the initial overtures.

It was Nick Green's colleague (and indeed wife) Sam, a quondam BBC *Watchdog* presenter, who had come up with the idea of sending me the bear. A low blow.

Once around the table with Nick I was, as Sam had no doubt anticipated, hooked, netted, gutted, filleted and ready for the table in no time at all. Lo's first impression had not been inaccurate. Nick is both enthusiastic and nice. Enthusiastic to the point of mania. To have a meeting with Nick Green is to be sucked into a vortex of zeal, zip and unquenchable zest that is more than just a sensational score at Scrabble. Before I quite knew what I was doing I was sitting in the doctor's surgery being filled to the brim with immunising doses of

hepatitis, yellow fever, typhoid and tetanus.

My only previous experience in the field of documentary had been as part of a Comic Relief film in Africa called *Letter From Mandela*. I had interviewed orphans whose parents had been killed by AIDS and travelled to the Bwindi National Park in Uganda to look at some mountain gorillas before handing over the baton to Geri Halliwell at a place called (appropriately enough for that brand of Spice Girl) Ginja, where the Nile has its source. From this experience I had discovered that documentary films have very little to do with the presenter, who is a mixture of foreground dressing and background voice. The films belong to the producer, to the director, to camera and to sound: probably in that order, although this analysis will offend everybody except producers.

The spine of our film in Peru turned out to be the story of Yogi, a bear that had been captured by the people of a small village high in the Andes. Somehow Nick Green had arranged for us to take possession of this bear, who had lived in a tiny cage, barely large enough to allow him to turn around, for two years. In exchange for mattocks, grain, footballs and assorted Paddingtonia the village gave us Yogi.

From this village we put a tranquillised Yogi on an old Soviet helicopter and took him to a new enclosure in Aguas Calientes, the town that sits at the bottom of Peru's greatest man–made treasure, Machu Picchu.

This was the beginning of our obsession with Spectacled Bears and their destiny. We (and by 'we' I mean primarily Nick, in whose slipstream I am borne breathless along: Nick who has led this initiative from first to last and without whose demonic energy and enterprise nothing would ever have been done) decided within a week or so of returning to England that another programme should be made devoted this time entirely to the Spectacled Bear and that a charitable foundation should be established for the purpose of rescuing distressed bears, purchasing land for their exclusive use and to pursue research into their numbers, their habitat, behaviour and future.

None of this would have been possible of course without the encouragement of the BBC. They liked the Paddington film and were happy to commission this real live bear idea. That is why the name of Lorraine Heggessy, Controller of BBC One, is included in the list of names under the heading Acknowledgements at the end of this book. Whatever one may think of the current state of the BBC (an institution, like Woody Allen, endlessly under analysis, there is no doubting the power of its name. The words 'We are from OR Media, a small independent production company based in Chiswick' do not carry quite the same weight around the world as the magical incantation, 'We are from the BBC.' Mind you, this is a double-edged sword. To say 'We are from the BBC' is also to say, so far as officials and minor functionaries the world over are concerned, 'Please hold us upside down and help yourself to the money that pours in an endless stream from our bloated western pockets.' It is very hard to persuade anybody that the BBC's fame is more or less in inverse proportion to its budgetary largesse. Not that we are complaining.

I have wandered from strict chronology. On our return from the first visit to Peru, programme number two was commissioned. A month after the broadcast of *Paddington Bear: The Early Years* we were back in Peru for *Stephen Fry and the Spectacled Bears*.

I had decided that I would try and keep a fairly detailed diary this time. I diarise anyway, but strictly not for publication. The *Sunday Telegraph* had expressed an interest in publishing something on Peru and its bears and had offered a handsome fee which would help kick start the Foundation. Since I lost many years ago the ability to hold a pen, I knew that I would be relying on enough electricity to keep a Powerbook alive, but this would only be a problem in the more out of the way locations on our itinerary. The real problem would be another kind of energy altogether. After a long day's filming, especially at the kind of altitudes one meets in Peru, the first thing you want to do is have dinner with the crew and drink sufficient wine or Pisco to knock you out completely, leaving just enough life in your limbs to enable you to make it up to your room. The last thing you want to do is sit at a keyboard and type. The words have a habit of floating and dancing six inches in front of their real place on the screen. It was going to be, in other words, more a question of will-power than AC power.

---

ii

In which Peru is described. Something of that nation's history. We meet Alberto Fujimori, a case study in Peruvian history. A few facts concerning Spectacled Bears.

The *CIA World Fact Book*, that inestimable source of data on nation states, reveals that Peru covers 1,285,220 sq km ('slightly smaller than Alaska', they claim: to put this in perspective for the British reader the entire land mass of the United Kingdom is 244,280 sq km which the CIA describes as 'slightly smaller than Oregon'), shares a border with Chile, Bolivia, Brazil, Colombia and Ecuador, has a Pacific coastline 2,414 km long and boasts a population of some 27 and a half million (as of July 2001). The national flag is pleasantly described in modern heraldic English: 'three equal, vertical bands of red (hoist side), white, and red with the coat of arms centred in the white band; the coat of arms features a shield bearing a llama, cinchona tree (the source of qui-nine), and a yellow cornucopia spilling out gold coins, all framed by a green wreath'.

The capital, seat of government and largest city is Lima. The country's main natural resources are copper, silver, gold, petroleum, timber, fish, iron ore, coal, phosphate, potash and hydropower. The chief natural hazards that threaten the country – and few nations on earth are more threatened by nature than poor old Peru – include earthquakes, tsunamis, flooding, landslides and what the *World Fact Book* calls 'mild volcanic activity', the accuracy of which description is fervently prayed for by the people of Peru's second city, Arequipa, who suffered an earthquake in 2001 and live in the shadow of South America's best known active volcano El Misti, which many geologists believe to be overdue a Big One.

Given the CIA's record in world affairs, it may be that none of these data are reliable: that is a matter we must all judge for ourselves.

An indisputable fact about Peru is its variety of terrain. It has cause to consider itself the most naturally diverse nation on earth. The geographer's technical terms include words like antiplano, costa, selva, littoral, transmontane, cloud forest, semi-moist Amazonian rain forest, and the like. In terms a twenty-first-century human might better understand, this means you can travel eastwards by air in just two hours from a Pacific coastline, over the driest desert in the world (in some cases where there has been no significant rainfall since the last Ice

Age), thence over Scottish highland and Alpine style glens and valleys, followed by high plateaux or pampas and then massive towering peaks that glisten like alabaster in freezing sub-zero temperatures. As you pass over these Andes, the second highest mountain range in the world, the world beneath you drops away and in half an hour's flying time you are on the fringes of nature's Last Word: Amazonia. Within this, Planet Earth's lung, are contained (in Peru's southern jungle alone) 10 per cent of the world's entire population of birds. You might pass over either Lake McIntyre, the ultimate source of the River Amazon, which doesn't arrive at the sea for another six thousand kilometres at its Brazilian mouth, or Lake Titicaca, the world's highest navigable lake. All this in a journey many times shorter than that from Darwin, say, to Sydney, which would take you over nothing but relentlessly identical miles of what they call the GABA, the Great Australian Bugger All. This is not to dismiss Australia, a beautiful country, but to explain the unique qualities of Peru.

All this magnificence under the stewardship of a population of 27 and a half million whose per capita GDP is estimated by the CIA to be $4,500 (as opposed to Britain's $22,800, Germany's $23,400 or the United States of America's $36,200: all figures as of the year 2000). In 1999 the worst el niño in living memory did incomparable damage to Peru's economy and infrastructure: there is little reason to suppose that another disastrous weather system won't be along soon.

All this might seem to be running away from the main subject under advisement: the Spectacled Bear. Well, bear with me (no puns are intended or allowed on the subject of bears – they're too easy and bears themselves are offended by them) for a moment. Bears, being high up in the food chain and the largest mammal in the country, are what is known as an Index Species. The fate and health of the bear is a kind of barometer of the well-being and destiny of the entire ecosystem they inhabit. If the bear flourishes in other words, then the water-beetle, the condor and the passion-flower flourish.

Perhaps the ultimate question for anyone concerned with The Environment and all that it entails is this: how prosperous does a country have to be before it starts to spend money on its ecological well-being? We can all rehearse the argument that ecological and economical well-being are interdependent, but anyone save an unimaginative fanatic will accept that until there is an abundance of food on the human table, the bird table is going to remain bare. Can we expect Peruvians to turn their attention to the care of their boundless variety of habitats and terrains, when they are still crippled by debt, doubt and deprivation? They may hold ten thousand dollars-a-plate dinners in Beverly Hills to save their rare snowy owls and threatened fritillaries, but to expect the same in Lima is, obviously, ridiculous. It is all very well to tell a sovereign nation that it is in its best interests to care for its wildlife and forests and rivers – they know that, they are not idiots. But when they are facing internal terrorism, hyperinflation, corruption and staggering poverty it would be worse than naïve to expect ecology to be high on their list of priorities.

The bear knows nothing of this. He knows when he is pushed further and further out of the fertile highland slopes that have been his natural birthright. He knows when he has been shot by a farmer protecting his maize and fruit crops. Of high politics, unless we've all been missing something very important, the bear knows nothing.

Politically Peru, like many South American countries, boasts a lamentable record of instability: *coups d'état*, juntas, border wars and revolutions have caused greater devastation to the economy and environment than all the natural disasters in its history. One of the most merciless and violent terrorist organisations mankind has seen, the *sendero luminoso* or Shining Path, a Maoist guerrilla organisation of stunning ruthlessness (they were not above sending children into hotels with explosives strapped to their bodies) flourished, if that's quite the word, in the seventies and eighties, casting a shadow of terror over the whole land and setting back tourism and inward investment at a time when it was most needed. The Shining Path was largely defeated in the early nineties by Alberto Fujimori's government.

The example of Fujimori says much about Peru.

Swept to power in 1990, beating the Peruvian novelist Mario Vargas Llosa in a run-off round of voting by 24 per cent, this son of Japanese immigrants was born in Lima in 1938 (though this is subject now to some doubt – it is possible he was in fact born in Japan, which would have barred him from standing for presidential election in the first place). A gifted man with two academic degrees, one in Agrarian Economics and one in Mathematics, he rose to national fame as a political analyst on television before founding his own party Cambio 90 (*cambio* is the Spanish for change, as anyone who has ever tried to cash a traveller's cheque on holiday will know). He inherited a country wracked by corruption, economic chaos, guerrilla warfare and drug trafficking. Fujimori 'instituted reforms intended to retain a free-market system and appeal to international lenders. He deregulated and decentralized the economy, cut government operating costs by 10 per cent, cut tariffs, liberalized foreign exchange rates, ordered all state-owned companies to raise their prices to profitable market rates, deregulated airlines, trucking and long-distance bus travel, streamlined procedures for registering businesses and eased import restrictions. The inflation rate began to slow and, within a year, had stabilized at 139 per cent' (source: CNN).

What could be rosier? Inflation down to a mere 139 per cent. Not only that, but Fujimori all but defeated the Shining Path, capturing the leader Guzman in 1992 and shattering its infrastructure with a policy of retribution against sympathisers and harbourers of terrorists that almost matched the Shining Path itself in its ferocity. On the basis of this twin victory against hyperinflation and hyperterrorism Fujimori won a landslide return to power in 1995 and then, with his popularity waning as the economy began to slide again, took the decision to stand for a third (constitutionally illegal) term. By this time he had become just another authoritarian tin-pot dictator, relying on his shadowy 'security adviser' Vladimiro Montesinos to keep tabs on his political, journalistic and academic opponents with a series of increasingly dirty tricks. All this culminated in Fujimori fleeing Peru for Japan in 2000, where now he hides (a hero to the Japanese who will not give him up) evading charges of state embezzlement running into (it is claimed) over a billion dollars ransacked from the public treasury. Montesinos is at the time of writing under arrest, facing charges relating to what Peruvians, with some amusement, call the 'Vladi Video' scandal: hours of videotaped evidence revealing massive pay-offs from hundreds of now disgraced officials, financiers and industrialists.

Still, he has his supporters: one startlingly hagiographical biography, *The President Who Dared To Dream*, advertises itself thus:

This is the compelling story of Alberto Fujimori. He

*is a special person, a Latin American leader and the
son of Japanese immigrants, Alberto is the link
between two cultures and from the blood of that link
which flows in his veins, he has reaped the best and
created the 'Peruvian miracle'. Because of him, millions of forgotten people in Peru for whom there will
never be a suit and tie, have a future again. What
was a dream for President Alberto Fujimori when he
became president of politically, socially and economi-
cally ravaged Peru in 1990 has become a reality. He
is indeed 'The President Who Dared to Dream'.*

Mm … I dwell on this history of Fujimori because it
seems to me in many ways to present a condensed history of Peru that is closer to the destiny of Spectacled
Bears than you might think. From disaster to promise
back to disaster again, by way of hope, violence, corruption and incompetence. Certainly the country is more
prosperous than it was in 1990 and certainly therefore,
the bears might be thought to have a brighter future
than before. Yet with prosperity come greater markets
for crops and a greater need to cultivate more and more
land. Prosperity, Janus-like, presents ecology with two
faces – one benign and one malignant.

  That is enough on political animals: let us turn to animal animals. The Spectacled Bear, *tremarctos ornatus* of
the family *Ursidae*, is the only bear native to South
America. They are officially classed as carnivores, but

this is a confusing taxonomical anomaly that says more about zoologists than bears, since they are almost exclusively eaters of fruits, cereals, succulents, cacti and bromeliads (spiny fruity plants like the pineapple). Because they will also munch on an ant from time to time, they are described as meat-eaters. Devourers of flesh who also nibble the odd blade of grass do not get classified as herbivores, but that is something for biologists to explain.

The Spectacled Bear inhabits the coastal and inland deserts, dry forest, rain forest, cloud forest, steppe, and paramo of Ecuador, Peru, Colombia, Bolivia and possibly Brazil, usually at altitudes between 1,900m and 2,350m. They have been seen as far south as the Bolivian/Argentine border and as far north as the Colombian/Panamanian border, though few believe there are resident populations in either Panama or Argentina. They are at their most populous on the eastern slopes of the Andes that run down from Ecuador through Peru to northern Bolivia.

Their name derives from the yellowish markings around the eyes that become more accentuated with maturity in both sexes. To sight them is a rarity for several reasons: they are mostly nocturnal, sleeping by day and foraging by night. They have a magnificent sense of smell and are excessively shy, which means they will have detected the presence of Man a long time before Man will have detected the presence of Bear. We heard, during our time in Peru, several stories of experienced natural history film-makers who had spent six months following tracks and droppings, only to retire beaten without a single frame of bear-rich footage.

What threatens them most directly? Well, panda.org, the official WWF International website, is filled with grisly information on this subject. An international trade in Spectacled Bear gall-bladders exists catering for the – you've guessed it – oriental market. As a matter of passing interest, Fujimori is one of those who makes great claims for Chinese medicine, that charming pro-curer of rhino horn and tiger livers. I anticipate letters from supporters of this branch of medicine telling me what a kindly practice it is, and how it works in har-mony with nature. Phooey. A few good results with atopic eczema do not excuse the engendering of a trade in the innards of rare creatures.

The major threat to the bears is of course the increas-ing depredation made upon their habitat by smallhold-ers, miners, farmers and – since the development of new strains of wet-climate coca – drug cartels. All the countries that host bear populations have National Parks, but they are enormous and hugely understaffed. Fourteen of the forty-two parks that contain bears are over a quarter of a million hectares in size. There is, according to the WWF, an average of just one guard for every half million acres of parkland. In the Rio Las Piedras park in the huge Manu reservation in Peru, oil drilling has wrecked an enormous swathe of bear habitat. And remember, bear habitat is habitat shared by hundreds of thousands of other species too. At least half the parks comprising bears have now been infiltrated by the drug trade with the obvious consequence that they are now functionally no go areas for all but the suicidal.

It is also true, as we discovered, that the organisation, management and morale of INRENA (the body that supervises the park of Peru) does not inspire confidence. In speaking of the parks, the WWF says, 'some lack the necessary management or political will needed to successfully maintain them'. I think that is putting it tactfully (we will ignore the split infinitive). This is not to blame those 'on the ground', who are for the most part dedicated and overworked. The key phrase is 'political will'.

Perhaps the most important fact for our purposes is phrased this way by the WWF: 'In many range countries, there is confusion and little concurrence on where boundaries are, let alone on whether bears reside in Parks or if Parks have conservation value for bears.'

It is this very confusion, arising from the startling lack of serious research on the animals, that first emboldened us to formulate the idea of a Bear Rescue Foundation (registered charity number 1092717).

Lincoln Park Zoo in California has done important work on breeding habits and keeps the International Stud Book on Spectacled Bears, which intriguing sounding volume is an indispensable resource for tracking bloodlines, genetic properties and similar important data. Other organisations within and without the bear's host countries have done work, but if you compare the amount of archival information available on them to that on mountain gorillas, tigers or rhinos, for example, it is easy to see that this is one of earth's most massively under-researched mammals.

Our own website, written by the redoubtable Mike Matson of Apple, of whom more within the body of the book, can be found at www.bear-rescue.tv, and we would be delighted by a visit from you.

---

iii

Presenting the personnel behind Stephen Fry and the Spectacled Bears *the BBC documentary. Comprising a word or two on the subject of film-making.*

The crew and personnel for the film *Stephen Fry and the Spectacled Bears* were the same (with the exception of the editor) as that assembled for the making of *Paddington Bear: The Early Years*.

Camera: John Warwick. A man of vast experience and monumental patience. In order to be a successful cameraman for documentaries of the kind we were making you need to be able to walk for miles and miles with a heavy camera on your shoulders and to have developed a visual and narrative instinct that only experience and natural aptitude can provide. John has an almost Zen quality of stillness and patience. His belief is that the stories and pictures come to the camera that waits and watches and avoid the camera that busies itself to seek them out.

Sound: Tim White. Technical expertise to the (self-confessed) point of nerdiness, combined again with years of varied experience. Sound is usually the forgotten medium in documentary film-making. If you notice it, it's probably failing, but if it's not properly recorded and integrated into the final cut the visual experience is compromised. Tim was the man with the right sized screwdriver and the correct battery for every occasion where such things were needed. Aside from his formidable qualities as a recordist he was indispensable to me as a repairer of spectacles and fellow Mac enthusiast.

Direction: Alan Lewins. Alan's BAFTA nominated documentary on the history of the popular song, *Walk On By*, tells you something about his versatility. A quite unflappable man, and perhaps the most fantastically disorganised packer of luggage the world has ever known, Alan like most good directors I have encountered in any genre carries most of his ideas in his head, only occasionally committing them to shot-lists or scenarios. The nature of documentary is such that the producer will have planned an itinerary of locations which are more or less fixed, due to permissions to film, flight plans, availability of interviewees and so on. The director, within these constrictions, has to be open and flexible as to the unfolding developments of the day. If you are halfway up a mountain there is naturally a fixed amount of tape carried up there with you, as well as a limited number of battery packs to power camera and sound equipment. The skill is to pace the filming through the day, knowing when you need the presenter on camera, when general views (GVs) will be of value in the edit, with later narration to be devised and when all the shots he needs have been captured. The director also works hard in post-production, in Alan's case providing me, after the first edit, with a script to put into my own words which will eventually serve as the voice-over narration for the film.

Production: I have already told you something about the human dynamo Nick Green. He looks like a teenage matinée idol, talks like a man who has been told his vocal cords have only a week left to live and remains cheerful in the face of setbacks which would have Pollyanna throwing furniture and sobbing with frustration. He is far more experienced than you would think to look at him, having made his bones on such BBC stalwarts as *Watchdog* and *Holiday*. In the months preceding our involvement Nick travelled (with Juan Tirado of whom more below) back and forth between London and Peru setting up all the dates and locations for the shoot. It is always hard to explain, in any entertainment medium, precisely what a producer is. They are in charge of the money, but it isn't usually theirs – though I suspect Nick is personally out of pocket as far as the whole Peruvian adventure is concerned, having donated a very generous sum of money to the Bear Rescue Foundation as well as greasing a few palms in Peru with his own funds. Producers hire the main personnel (but usually allow the director to choose sound and camera) and supervise the budget and the itinerary. They are adjutant, sergeant major, paymaster general and strategic staff officer all rolled into one. They have to remember whose names should go on the credits, check any legal considerations such as libel and copyright clearances, liaise with the broadcaster (the BBC in our case) and … well, in short they have to remember and think of everything. At home producers are often complemented by assistants, secretaries, associate and co-producers. In the field, if one can glamorise location filming thus, budgetary necessity forces them to do everything themselves. If it sounds as though I am hero-worshipping Nick, then I probably am. The rest of the crew would say to each other, throughout our time in

Peru. 'Thank God I'm not a producer. I'd rather shovel shit for a living.' It became a kind of mantra for us.

Stills: At a time when everyone has a digital camera and the concomitant capacity to clog up internet bandwidth with travel photographs and shots of their genitals it is worth bearing in mind that nothing yet outperforms old-fashioned emulsion and a chemical bath. Rob Fraser, who is responsible for the photographs in this book, was with us throughout our travels, accompanied by his partner Polly Sheesby. I think you will see that the difference between a snapshot and a professional photograph is not unlike the difference between a beach sandcastle and the Mont St Michel.

Our Man From Peru: We were fortunate enough throughout both our visits to Peru to have the services of Juan Tirado as a co-producer and Local Liaison Officer. Juan rose through the ranks of the Peruvian Diplomatic Service and served his country in embassies around the world. If you are going to film in a distant country whose bureaucracy is not always friendly or comprehensible then have with you a man with a diplomatic passport, a man who knows where the bodies are buried, a man whose address book contains the telephone numbers of cabinet ministers and senior civil servants, a man of infinite resource, tact, guile and humour.

Presenter/Narrator: This is where I come in. Most of the credit accrues to the one whose face and voice take the viewer on the journey, yet he is the member of the crew who does the least work. I am not attempting false modesty here; it is a fact. While the other members of the crew are involved with every single shot, the presenter often finds himself unwanted. The director needs as much footage as he can get of the locations visited and much of this takes the form of General Views of townscapes, countryside and so on. At other times the need for close-up shots taken from the point of view of the presenter will arise. In these GVs and POVs, as they are known, the presenter's face and person are, by definition, not required. Sometimes you are needed in shot as a piece of set-dressing, present but silent. It was often my job to tag along and stand where I was told while the crew got on with it. There are however moments where what is called for is a Piece To Camera, a bit of chat that sets or sums up the scene. The knack of documentaries of this kind, it seems to me, is to judge when a piece-to-camera is required and when the film is best served by footage uncontaminated by on-site verbals. After all, once you're back home, all kinds of information can be given the viewer in the form of narration over film. Flexibility is all. Since we all got on with each other well enough not to worry about egos I never felt afraid to suggest a piece-to-camera at any given moment. 'Oh look, there's a cocoa tree. Shall I do a piece-to-camera about chocolate?' That sort of thing.

Since I had the most free time of anyone, it seemed a reasonable idea to keep a journal during filming. It is this diary that forms the basis of the book you are holding in your hands. Beyond tidying up unacceptable mistakes I have not revised the text in any substantial way.

  I hope this book may inspire you to travel to Peru. For all my moaning about bureaucracy and enteric explosions, it is the most beautiful country you will ever visit. Whether you stay in five-star luxury or travel as a backpacker on the Inca Trail, you will have, as I did, the time of your life. And now, at least, you will be able to visit at least one couple of love-struck Spectacled Bears on your way to Machu Picchu. Give them my warmest regards and a ripe avocado. If you can't visit physically, point your browser to www.bear-rescue.tv.

———————

'An indisputable fact about Peru is its variety of terrain.

It has cause to consider itself the most naturally diverse nation on earth.'

2

Friday 11 January, 2002
Miraflores Park Hotel, Lima, Peru

The smelliest tailor in the world has just left my room. With characteristic inefficiency I failed to bring with me to Peru a suit which Nick Green, our amiable young producer, had reminded me on at least seventeen occasions on no account to forget. There is to be a ceremony here at which Michael Bond will be recognised by the full panoply of the state for services to Peru. It seems that I too will receive some form of gift, which is gratifying, if a spot bewildering. Michael Bond created Peru's most famous citizen (to non-Peruvians at least); I have done nothing more than chronicle the bear's supposed background for a BBC documentary, but I was never one to look a gift-bear in the mouth.

 I also neglected smart shoes. All I have are stout outdoor climbing boots with soles like the tread of a Tonka toy and some rather breezy sandals, neither of which will do when the First Lady, for it will be she, bestows upon me the Order of the High Andes or whatever it is that I am to receive. Nick Green and the very kind Marisa behind the desk here at the Miraflores Park Hotel made a large number of phone calls to *zapaterías* all over Lima and discovered that the highest size shoes go up to in Peru is 45. Since I can barely jam my big toe into anything smaller than a 48 this caused great alarm. We do not want to show disrespect by having me shuffle up the aisle of the Presidential Palace shod like a Woodstock hippy. I made a rather frantic call to Jo, my PA in England, asking her to DHL some respectable foot-joy to Lima forthwith. It being Friday, however, it seems that neither Fed-Ex, nor TNT nor DHL nor anybody else will pick up a parcel or a package from any other location than the office of a registered company. Nor will they suffer such a parcel or package to be delivered to their depot. Jo lives in Norwich. Perhaps the problem might not arise in London. In any case it means that I shan't have the shoes for a day or so. So much for 'when it absolutely positively has to be there' and 'aint no mountain high enough' and other such promises made in courier company commercials. It amused the offices of DHL-stroke-TNT-stroke-Fed-Ex to be told that a pair of shoes had to be planed to Lima ASAP – I suppose their East Anglian branches don't often get such requests – but it didn't alter their dogged adherence to 'company policy' one tiny drop.

In the meantime, my size presenting just as much a challenge to the off-the-peg gent's outfitters of the town, a tailor has visited my room. I am sorry to say that he combines the worst kind of halitosis with an even fouler style of body odour, resulting in a combination which hangs about the room hours after he has gone. I know this sounds unlikely but it is absolutely true. The stench would seem to penetrate the curtains, the fabric of the furniture, the wallpaper, everything. Even with the windows open and the air-conditioning blasting out its highest setting the miasma refuses to clear. There's a well-known British actress whose name I shall naturally keep to myself who is famous for the pungent horror of her body odour. It is so terrible that dressers on films, theatre and television have to be paid extra to work with her. I promise I'm not making this up. She did a TV drama not long ago and the costume hire company burned all the clothes when they were returned. After three boil washes they still stank to hell. She's exceptionally nice and no one has told her, which I suppose is right. How can you break such news to someone, even kindly? Of course, it's possible all this is said about me… one never knows. I know I can pong a bit after a sweaty day's filming and I've never been much of a deodorant man, regarding them as somehow non-U and not quite the thing, but if I were to find out that all these years I had been talked about like this actress I think I'd want to end it all.

It's been a rather false dawn here at the Miraflores, a frantically luxurious Orient Express Group hotel, the best in Lima. Nick Green and I arrived on Tuesday to do a little planning and we shan't fly up to Trujillo to start filming till Sunday – well, Nick has been doing the planning, I have been stuck in my suite writing an introduction to a posthumous collection of Douglas Adams's writings and enjoying the free broadband internet connection piped into every room. The crew, cameraman John, soundman Tim and director Alan, arrive this evening.

There are certain naughty advantages to hanging around in a country like Peru. You can buy anything you like at pharmacies, from Tamazepam to Viagra and all stops in between, so I have been stocking up on Losec and Zopiclone, my proton-pump inhibitors and sleeping-pills of choice respectively. A proton-pump inhibitor, in case you're thinking of something quite dreadful, is nothing worse than a kind of supercharged antacid and since I suffer from a dreadful thing called a hiatus hernia which causes scorching acid reflux every time I try and get to sleep (thus counteracting even the most liberal doses of Zopiclone) it's useful to have a cheap and inexhaustible supply of what otherwise costs a lot of money and endless visits to the doctor. The older you get the more a good night's sleep counts.

Location filming however comes down to two essentials even more crucial than sleep: Bowels and laundry.

I have no doubt I will have more to say on those luminous topics as the three weeks unwind. So far, of course, so good. We're in a first class hotel with bottled water, good food and a splendid housekeeping service. Whether I will have been able to keep my temper and usual sunny outlook on life when we have been living the life of a New Zealand backpacker or gap-year eco-warrior is another matter.

The sun dips quite fast over the yardarm this close to the equator and from my picture window I see it dropping into the Pacific like a cocktail cherry into a high-ball glass which reminds me that it is approaching the hour of the Pisco Sour. Pisco is the Peruvian drink. There is coca tea of course and *chicha*, made from *maíz morado*, a purple corn and its grown-up cousin *chicha de Jora* which is fermented with the help of the spittle of the mountain people who make it – yummeee – but Pisco is to Peru what whisky is to Scotland and bourbon to Tennessee. It's basically a kind of grappa or marc: the white *quebranta* grape, the constituent of the best 'pisco puro', makes foully insipid wine but a marvellous fiery spirit. Pisco itself is a small town in the Ica province in the south, halfway between Lima and Nasca. The Spaniards brought the first vines to Peru in the seventeenth century from the Canary Isles and viti-culture became so successful here that the King of Spain banned the import of popular colonial wine, which was hurting the domestic wine growers. Pisco is most popularly presented in the form of a frothing sour: lemon or lime juice, sugar (though Pisco purists prefer cane syrup) and egg white with a little dot of cinnamon or angostura plopped into the middle. Delicious and invigorating. I shall shower and toddle down to the Jekyll and Hyde Bar. There is a snooker room there so perhaps a frame or two before dinner. The rigours of the explorer's life.

'Amongst all this Peruvian flora and fauna shyly lurks the almost wholly unknown Spectacled Bear.'

Saturday 12 January, 2002
Miraflores Park Hotel, Lima

This is the kind of diarrhoea that you read about in horror novels. I have tried to start today's entry three times, but on each occasion have been forced to my luxurious bathroom to do far from luxurious things. It's my own fault, naturally. First of all I shouldn't have discoursed with such blithe authority on the subject of bowels and laundry. Such hubris was bound to result in something appalling. My laundry returned this morning in fine order and a cute leather-strapped rush basket of the kind favoured only by peasants and the super-rich. A breakfast meeting this morning with a man from the Peruvian Ministry of Agriculture seemed to go well – until he left. The official was concerned that our film might show Peru in a less than favourable light as far as its treatment of bears is concerned. We are travelling to Huaraz tomorrow to rescue two mangy and miserable specimens that have been caged against the wall of a café for some years as an attraction for the patrons. The official is aware that the sight of them on camera will set all Britain in a rage. I assured him that I had planned (as indeed I had) to remind the British audience in a piece-to-camera, or in the post-production voice-over commentary, that our own indigenous population of bears was teased, tormented, tortured and danced into extinction many years ago and that we are in no position to cast the motes out of Peru's eye. I think I am right in saying that in Shakespeare's day there were more bear-pits than theatres in London. It's possible the bear in *A Winter's Tale* famous for his appearance in the stage direction *exit pursued by a bear* may well have been real.

The official seemed pleased by this and explained the enormous problems facing Peru. While Brazil is manifestly bigger, Peru contains the greatest number of different types of ecosystem in the world – 83 out of the 104 that make up the planet's biosphere. Don't ask me to name them all. The official doesn't expect us to make a 'Welcome to Peru, land of contrasts: here, all are contented and well-nourished as they go about their bright and prosperous day…' sort of propagandalogue, but he is legitimately worried about his country being portrayed as savagely unconcerned with its wildlife. They have a tenth of all the planet's bird species, let alone big cats like the puma and jaguar, monkeys, capybaras, giant otters, pink river dolphins, enormous viscacha rabbits, condor and the astonishing Puya Raimondi, perhaps the most remarkable and beautiful plant in the world whose monstrously phallic stamen can grow to forty feet in length. That list doesn't scratch the surface of this country's astounding diversity. The glaciers, the deserts, the islands, the highlands, canyons (the two deepest canyons on earth are in Peru – over *twice* the depth of the Grand Canyon), the Amazonian jungle, the high *altiplano*, the rain forest, rivers and coastline contain dazzling and rare life forms far beyond humanity's ability to specify or number. If you have a liking to see your name immortalised in Latin then go into *La Selva* (the jungle) north, south or west it hardly matters, place a white sheet on the ground beneath a tree and point upwards with an insecticide fogging machine. I guarantee a bug will fall into your sheet that is unknown to science. As Fuchs is memorialised in the fuchsia and Dahl in the dahlia, so will you be in your *scarabus blenkinsopia*. If the Peruvian government were as rich as the United States it would still have a hell of a problem on its hands combining the needs of a growing population with the awful privilege of standing guardian to this teeming Eden.

With all this on his plate, the last thing the official needs is a First World film crew inspiring the sentimental wrath of a British television audience. I tried to show that I understood his problem and that we would do our best to be fair and honest.

Amongst all this Peruvian flora and fauna shyly lurks the almost wholly unknown Spectacled Bear. Jacques Cousteau introduced the world to the pink dolphin or bufeo which many had believed to be extinct, we have all seen footage of condor, jaguar and capuchin monkeys, I narrated a BBC documentary on capybara a couple of years ago myself, but the Spectacled Bear remains almost entirely unphotographed and unstudied. We happened upon one in the course of our Paddington film and we have returned because we just felt somehow that the famous label around Paddington's neck was a call to help not just one South American bear, but the whole species. The Spectacled Bear serves as a signature breed, an index of the health of the entire system of systems that make up Peru. Our project is, we hope, something a little more than donkey sanctuary sentimentality. Nonetheless, sentiment if not sentimentality is unavoidable (at least for me) when dealing with such delightful creatures and I won't apologise for it.

I did my best to communicate something of our missionary zeal to the Ministry of Agriculture man and he appeared to be relieved. While we were talking I noticed out of the corner of my eye that Juan Tirado, our Peruvian born co-producer, adviser, counsellor and general smoother-over of problems, appeared jittery. Since Juan is about the most urbane, unruffled man you could ever hope to meet this puzzled me. He was trained in the diplomatic service, which is how he first came to Britain, now his home.

Once the man from the ministry had departed, the source of Juan's discomfort became clear. He had just heard news that Lima Zoo, which was to offer two bears from Santiago called Yogi and Boo-Boo hospitality for a few days, has suddenly decided it has no facilities and must build a cage from scratch for $4,000 dollars. Now please. In cash. This overnight 'realisation' flies in the face of an agreement arrived at three months ago to house our refugees and has a great deal to do with the fact that we are the BBC and therefore can, it is assumed, be bled white. This is how these people work: they leave it to the very last minute, when you are bereft of any other options, to come up with the sad shake of the head and the sorrowful announcement that money must be found for some new 'problem'. It's sickening. Corruption is first and last what holds Peru back from prosperity. It is often manifested as no more than a small block somewhere in the narrowest pipeline (in this case a minor zoo official lubriciously rubbing his fingers together and potentially destroying months of careful planning) but no matter how small the clog or how narrow the pipeline, the whole machine is clogged nonetheless. Of course the current President's predecessor, Alberto Fujimori, led by example and fleeced his nation of billions, so it isn't always a case of minor officialdom fouling the footpath. Juan's rage at the zoo's behaviour was something to behold: he loves his country deeply and simply cannot bear it when this kind of thing happens. I asked why he didn't immediately tell the official, who is after all responsible for Peru's national parks and conservation areas and might be goaded into instant action. 'I shall go over his head,' said Juan grimly, 'to the Minister himself.' I pray he gets a result or we won't be able to help these bears without paying the bribe and therefore contributing our own dollop of poison to the whole noxious cocktail of sleaze and malversion.

From this point on my day started to go wrong. My beloved iPod has gone blooey. I don't know what the problem is but it won't play any of the hundred and twenty hours' worth of music stored on it. I can play the tracks through the iPod on the computer, so the files are all there. I have the whole of Wagner's *Ring*, *Die Meistersinger*, *Don Giovanni*, *The Magic Flute*, scores of pop and jazz albums and, more importantly for my immediate purposes, eight hours of Michel Thomas's Spanish Course. I don't know if you're familiar with Michel Thomas: he taught Princess Grace to speak French and has a list of famous alumni that boggles the brain. I heard of him from Emma Thompson whom he taught Spanish a couple of years ago for a Chilean film project she had initiated. He's a survivor of Nazism, his family all perished in Auschwitz, and he has a unique and perfectly brilliant way of teaching languages. He can more or less guarantee to have you in command of a thousand-word vocabulary in a week or ten days. No homework, absolutely no writing down: you just listen. Anyway it would have been perfect tomorrow on an eight-hour drive to Huaraz to have his soothing, hypnotic tones humming hispanically into my ear driven by the magical little iPod.

I trailed miserably to the Larco Mar Centre (a sort of shopping centre that stunningly overhangs the Pacific) and decided to lunch at (and I blush here at my unadventurous naffness) Tony Roma's (*Famosa Por Su Costillas*... Famous For His Ribs), an American franchise restaurant probably owned by Pizza Hut or someone horrid. I had Chicken Caesar followed by Tenderloin Strip with bottled water and a frozen lemonade. Maybe it was the frozen lemonade, maybe it was the water the lettuce was washed in. In any case, I had hardly been back fifteen minutes before my bowels started griping like a Silesian fishwife. The very charming hotel staff had insisted on moving me from my very comfortable set of rooms to the Presidential Suite, where I had stayed in May of last year when making the Paddington documentary. I therefore had to hang around graciasing the bellboy as he transferred luggage from one suite to another and waiting for the business centre representative to find out that what I had said about the Ethernet connection in the room was true, i.e. that it was buggered: all the while my stomach seethed and bubbled like boiling jam and I wanted to scream at everyone to get out and leave me to the lavatory. The bellhop went, followed by the business centre girl, and my hand was just rounding about the handle of the bathroom door when there came a knock. Someone wanted to service the swimming pool on my

'The bellhop went, followed by the business centre girl, and my hand was just rounding about the handle of the bathroom door when there came a knock. Someone wanted to service the swimming pool on my balcony. I reveal all this information in the full knowledge that airy talk of Presidential Suites, private swimming pools and so on is likely to have a lot of you reaching for your pump action shotguns. It is the duty of the chronicler, however, to be honest and so honest I am being.'

balcony. I reveal all this information in the full knowledge that airy talk of Presidential Suites, private swimming pools and so on is likely to have a lot of you reaching for your pump action shotguns. It is the duty of the chronicler, however, to be honest and so honest I am being.

For those of you with reflex BBC-hatred, which I know covers many in Britain these days, you should know that this film, although to be shown on the BBC, is not a BBC production – they are paying the going rate to screen the thing, but OR Media, Nick Green's company, is making the film and paying all the bills, so you can acquit our Public Broadcasting Company of profligacy on this front at least. OR Media's profit would be larger if they put the crew up in some terrible flea-ridden hovel but Nick Green doesn't think like that. A happy crew is a good crew is his mantra and I'm with him one hundred per cent. What the hell, why am I trying to apologise? I'm staying in the Presidential Suite and it's great.

Except for the diarrhoea.

The buggered iPod.

The non-functional broadband connector.

'Look, a rainbow.
A sign from God!'

Monday 14 January, 2002
Casa de Pocha, Carhuaz and Yungay Viejo

We travelled yesterday. God how we travelled: from ten o'clock to nine in the evening over precipitous gorges and screamingly dangerous mountain bends that made *The Italian Job* look like a cosy tool through broad leafy lanes. We laid by in the outskirts of Lima while the vet travelling with us, Pável Cartagena, waited for a woman to come and dispense the necessary tranquillisers, syringes and medicines required for the betterment of the bears we are to visit. The route then took us up the Pan American Highway, a road that, as the name might suggest, could deliver us, were we in the mood, all the way up to Alaska. Huaraz and Carhuaz seemed far enough. Today we are to visit Yungay, scene of the appalling earthquake and avalanche that accounted for up to eighty thousand lives in 1970, one of the worst human catastrophes in living memory.

We are staying in the Casa de Pocha, a remarkable hostel that just happens to belong to the sister of Rocío, a fixer-cum-guide who is accompanying us for most of our journey. Pocha is Rocío's sister. Twenty-one years ago she was impregnated by an Italian scoundrel of whom she does not speak. Being of high-born Liman (they say *Limeño* or *Limeña*) stock she betook herself here to Huaraz to escape the censure of her family and rebuild her life. A son was born and a house built, brick by brick, slate by slate, beam by beam. All the work of her own hands.

It is of unbelievable beauty: the whole place writhes with animal life, there is a marvellous brown alpaca (never got a chance to photograph him) whose wool Pocha takes once a year to make all manner of woven objects, there are dogs, cats, hens, geese, goats and a cow for the milk.

All the food here is from her land, grown biodynamically and without chemicals. The former principle, biodynamic husbandry, was made apparent last evening since we had a *luna nueva*, an important moment for those who plant and harvest according to the cycles of the moon. The cooking is done by day with the help of two large silvery collectors that incongruously look like satellite dishes in which water boils in a matter of two and a half minutes.

For the evenings they use the simplest wood-burning stove you could imagine and what electricity there is comes from a rickety old generator. I fear for the battery life of my computer since we are to be here until Wednesday. The only power socket is in a shed somewhere and John's camera batteries and Tim's recorder cells naturally take precedence. There is of course no telephone. A drying room uses the heat of the sun:

slices of mango lie on a table like ready-made desktop wallpaper.

My own room is a simple whitewashed affair, arrived at through rough stable type doors. There is a lavatory, a table, a chair, two candles and a window.

The bed was made for me last week when word arrived that I was a giant. When I say the bed was made, I don't mean that sheets were put upon it, I mean the bed was made. Manufactured. Actually made. This is very touching but I am beginning to tire of the message that Peru sends out to me. You Are A Freak, Señor Free, as they like to call me. Somehow Pocha managed to get to Huaraz where there is a ten-seat cinema (or room with television and video player as we would call it). She watched *Wilde* there some time ago and told me that she intended to put a plaque above my bed saying 'Oscar Slept Here'.

Pocha's son, now twenty-one, is the hero and acknowledged dish of the area. He is away, teaching Chileans how to operate a kayak properly. Apparently he has for some years been in great demand as a model, his startling beauty being one of the wonders of the district. I am to be shown photographs this evening. He grew up in this magical place, helping build, milking cows and taking work as soon as he was able as a white-water rafting instructor (they say the kayaking here is the best in the world, covering every grade of difficulty, danger and beauty), translator and hiking and archaeological guide. There are worse lives to lead in the world.

Something of a strange morning: Nick was in Huaraz dealing with the inevitable corruption. He had sent $400 to an official who was to set in train the business of feeding the two bears properly and preparing them for Pável, the vet. Naturally, the money had 'disappeared' much as enemies of the state once did. The bears are apparently in a worse condition than they were when Nick did a recce before Christmas. It is now considered vital to move them from where they are: the original plan was to build them a better cage and provide regular income for feeding them. No one now believes that the money will be used for that purpose, so the plan Nick concocted this morning was to have them transported to Lima Zoo (who had been so appalling about the Chilean bears we were going to move there). He returned at lunchtime fuming slightly, but as determined as ever to rescue those bears. In the meantime I had been reading on a hammock. Until you have seen (and heard) me attempting to mount and dismount a hammock your life has been nothing but a rehearsal. Think of a hippopotamus trying to ascend a rope ladder and you'll have a reasonably accurate picture. At lunch Nick told us all that had transpired in Huaraz. Pocha, scarcely looking up from her *estufa*, offered to look after the bears herself: so long as we provided the odd bit of money for their food and the materials for the construction of a cage, she would be

'Today we are to visit Yungay,
scene of one of the worst
human catastrophes in
living memory'

happy to do it. 'Do it' includes building the cage, nothing to a woman who has built a house. This is undoubtedly the best solution. The final years of their lives will be incomparably better than the last seventeen or so. The only other problem of the morning seemed to be the failure of the Mitsubishi minivan's transmission: since we need this to ferry us and equipment hither and yon, it's something of a blow. It worked well enough to take us to Yungay this afternoon but it's going to have to be fixed tonight.

Yungay then. After all I've written about Perudise and the magical and extraordinary beauty of this bulging Eden, it is natural that there should be a serpent. Yungay Viejo is a small town that nestles in the valley that runs between La Cordillera Negra and La Cordillera Blanca, the two chains of mountains that run north to south down the Pacific coast. The latter, as the name might imply, glistens with white mountains and is the great tourist attraction, a prominent stop on the gringo trail. Its greatest mountain is Huascarán, the highest peak in Peru. Two peaks in fact, *el pico sur* and *el pico norte*. Yungay was for many years a quiet but notably elegant township that sat in the valley happily going about its affairs. All that changed on 31st May 1970. At three twenty-three in the afternoon a mighty earthquake ripped the town in two. The event lasted an appalling 90 seconds and registered 7.9 on the Richter Scale. It did much damage to many other towns along the valley. Fate had something quite immensely terrible in mind for Yungay however. The force of the tremors caused a section of glacier at the side of *el pico norte* to dislodge itself. It moved down the mountain side, gathering incredible speed and millions of tons of rocks and ice as it cascaded. Within three minutes, from start to finish, the avalanche had travelled thirty kilometres until it came to rest. It came to rest on the flat valley floor. It came to rest on the town of Yungay. The town was no more. All that was left was a flat, lifeless inland beach of ice and rubble. In all, eighty thousand people lost their lives: more than Hiroshima and Nagasaki combined. There were survivors. Ninety-two people scrambled to the highest point in the town, the cemetery of all places. Even more fortunately, 394 children were visiting a circus in a nearby village.

We arrived this afternoon to film what remains nearly thirty-two years on. The major memorial is a vast Christ with outstretched arms looking across at Huascarán, his back to the tortoise-skin folds of *la cordillera negra*. The Christ stands, like a marzipan bridegroom decorating a cake, atop a three-tiered circular structure every inch of which contains a plaque that fronts a private vault. It's perhaps more like the base of a sporting trophy, but instead of the names of champions inscribed around each ring, there are the names of the dead.

They have rebuilt a simulacrum of the church at the

other end of the remains of the town, and in between church and cemetery white kerb-stones mark out where once were streets. Nature has grassed these over of course, so the town seems more like a park than a ruin. One remarkable sculpture turns out to be not a work of art but the genuine wreckage of a bus, the tangled steel embracing at its feet the round red flank of the wing of a Volkswagen Beetle.

The entrance to Yungay Viejo is achieved through two rose gardens that have flourished on the thousands of bones that lie beneath. I did my piece-to-camera by a rock in front of these, with the replica church and the base of Huascarán behind. Frustratingly the peaks were concealed by a mass of cloud.

After I'd done my bit, Alan the director and John the cameraman went off to film inserts of some of the things I had talked about. I sat with Tim the soundman and two enchanting children from Yungay Nuevo (it is the entirely fitting tradition that local children, who are taught all the details of the 31st May 1970 at school, act as guides for the tourists and *Limeños* who come here) watching the skies clear, when Tim noticed two men inside one of the larger personal memorials that are spaced about the area of the village (often of course sited on the very places where those memorialised had their houses or shops): the men were bringing out flowers to place in front of the monument; we fell into conversation. It turned out they were survivors. One had lost his parents, his six brothers and sisters, his nieces and nephews, his cousins… in all 26 of his 'flesh family' as they say here. He comes twice a year, once in December or January, once on the 31st May itself. He had been in Lima at the time of the disaster, his *compañero*, who lost seventeen, had been in Yungay until half an hour before its destruction. I interviewed them both, with Rocío acting as a translator. These men had lived with one of the worst cataclysms imaginable for over thirty years, alone, entirely bereft of any blood family.

As we finished the interview one of the men tapped me excitedly on the shoulder and pointed towards Huascarán. '*Mira!*' he said. '*Un arco iris. Una señal de Dios!*' '*Look, a rainbow. A sign from God!*'

What kind of sign from what kind of God it is hard to conceive. 'I won't visit death like this to you again, I promise. I shall stay my hand and punish only child-killers, torturers and the wicked.' Is that what He was saying? That would be a divine precedent to be welcomed, but as likely as a good harvest in Ethiopia and justice for all. But to see this rainbow, suspended between the remains of Yungay and the massive ice giant that had caused so much death and agony with one shrug of its shoulders, took away my breath and the breath of us all.

The higher parts of the north and south peaks to the left and right respectively were beginning to show as the cloud rolled away. No picture gives a sense of just how much more mountain is still hidden. Nowhere outside the Himalayas are there higher peaks than in the Andes. Maybe I am not 'sensitive', but the valley does not give off a sense of tragedy or doom. Some innocent places glower with malice or sadness, some terrible places hide their histories. Yungay felt to me like a pleasant meadow with an astounding backdrop. It took the rainbow to focus my mind on where I was and what had happened there.

We returned in sombre mood, caught in the programme maker's eternal moral quandary. We had filmed (with permission, naturally) something we had not expected, living witnesses to the depth of a terrible tragedy: we were therefore very pleased with our day, it would make 'good television'. On the other hand we had been in a Valley of Death which makes Balaclava look like a children's theme park. Instead of stopping and thinking, we had greedily pointed our camera and grabbed opportunities to 'Make TV'. The usual excuse is that millions can now know something of an obscenely under-reported and under-exposed calamity and that the dead are owed at least that. Hum. It is convenient as an argument, but the slightly unpleasant taste in the mouth lingers.

'A robin redbreast in a cage
Sets all heaven in a rage'

Tuesday 15 January, 2002
Caras and Casa de Pocha, Huaraz

I was awoken, as is my custom, by a fierce and urgent cock. No but really. Shush. It was indeed Pocha's proud rooster that wrenched me from dreams of Spanish irregular verbs this morning at a decent six forty-five ack emma. The plan was to see if the morning offered a clearer view of Huascarán as we drove past on our way to Caras, Where The Bears Are.

They call the locals who live on the hill above here at the C de P a name that takes one to Tintin or Flash Gordon, they are known as 'the thunder people'. This is because when there is a storm the thunder always, wherever the actual storm might be, seems through some freak of acoustics to come from this one place. They are credited with gifts of weather prediction and had told Pocha that it would be *muy bonito*. Indeed it was. The bus (newly mended) arrived a highly acceptable half an hour late, which is teutonically early to the Peruanos. The legendary *una hora latinoamericana* is nothing to *una hora peruana*. At one point during the Paddington film we got on a bus for what we were assured was a twenty-minute drive and did not dismount until four hours later. An open road, free of traffic. Endearing or maddening, according to mood and need.

As we bowled through the valley (we being Nick, Alan, John, Tim, Rob and Polly, Rocío, Pável and self), the two ranges, *negra* and *blanca* on either side glowered and sparkled respectively as if this was the first day they had heaved their way up to the sky. They believe here that Huascarán's two peaks will always be shrouded in some quantity of cloud, because the mountain is ashamed of what it did to the people of Yungay: this morning a few shreds flounced like angel hair around the midriffs of the peaks, but for the first time we could see how astonishing Yungay's situation really is. At first glance you might think the nevada is not a mountain but a huddle of clouds. It all seems too far away to pose a threat to this broad and innocent little glen. Nevertheless, three minutes from the dislodging of the cornice to total destruction.

After half an hour of filming the peaks in a kind of dazed, respectful silence (it is impossible to hate the mountain) we made our way to the Café Palmira in Caras (not to be confused with Huaraz, where we are staying). The guidebooks refer, accurately enough, to Caras as a charming and pleasant township, an attractive alternative for the gringo for whom Huaraz has become too touristy. One, at least, goes on to mention the Café Palmira, recommending its trout and remarking that there is a small zoo.

A small zoo.

Well, the zoo cannot be described as large, so thus far

perfectly fine. To describe Adolf Hitler as a former Chancellor of Germany would also tell the truth. But there is telling the truth and there is covering the facts. There is Accurate and there is Necessary and Sufficient. The menagerie that Señor Suarez, the patron of the Café Palmira, runs is an affront to God, man and – most especially – beast. There are capuchin monkeys in as tragically forlorn a state as you can imagine, scratching and bouncing in bare concrete cupboards. There is a condor.

  You read me right. A condor. One of God's best, the soaring bird of prey who rules the cañons of southern Perú (¡caramba! but these accents are getting to me… two extra keystrokes and I always mistype) usually accompanied by Discovery Channel pipes of Pan.

> *A robin redbreast in a cage*
> *Sets all heaven in a rage.*

So wrote William Blake. What he would have thought of a condor in a cage I can't imagine. Well, Blake was the kind of honest spirit who did not accord value to creatures according to size, so it is likely he would not have distinguished between the two, but it is hard for us lesser men not to feel that imprisoning a condor is as wicked a thing as a human can do. I don't know about all heaven but I was certainly in a rage. I wanted to lock Sr Suarez and his glacial wife in a cage and throw the

'Misery. Ursine misery.'

key into the Pacific, but we were here to film the bears, to medicate them, to prepare their cage for their eventual retirement to the Casa de Pocha. Whatever I did, Producer Nick told me, I must play nice with the Suarezes. Smile egregiously. Grin and spray compliments. Few people can do egregious better than myself, I am assured on all sides, and I did not disappoint. I was a little mollified by the information that the condor had in fact been raised from an egg and that he had never flown. It was hard to claim that he looked in a bad state like the monkeys or the bears, of whom more in a moment.

Nonetheless, eh?

On the bears. These two sad creatures, both female, are María and Anita, in order of size. They were bought by Suarez from a poacher and he has kept them at the Palmira for the last eighteen years. Some kind of tick has given them a scabies-like infection in their lower halves which they have scratched bald, especially the smaller Anita, who scrabbled frantically at her skin from the moment she came up to greet us until the moment she was tranquillised.

Misery. Ursine misery. They have lived their lives and there is little we can do for them but move them to a grass-floored cage with foliage and the kind of amenities that we provided for Yogi, the bear that we met when we first visited Peru to make the Paddington film.

I did a piece-to-camera explaining what we were about to do while the bears grunted unhelpfully in the background. The first task then was to cut a hole with wire-cutters (well Pável the vet snipped and I helped) while the bears were distracted by carrots at the far corner. A large carrying cage with sliding door was placed against the new opening and the business of coaxing one of the bears into its temporary quarters began. Anita followed a trail of doped chocolate into the cage and we dropped the sliding door down. María watched this with great concern, warbling in her throat like a bird in distress. Her friend and constant companion of eighteen years had, for the first time ever, *ever*, disappeared. Just gone. Swallowed up into a battered eau de nil box. Earlier, when alarmed by the wire-cutting, they had hugged each other. Standing up, plantigrade as I believe the term is, they had embraced and gabbled to each other like anxious lovers about to be separated at the prison gates. Now María was alone, the outraged whoops and gurgles of her companion came plainly to her ears and half of her wanted to join Anita and the other half wanted nothing whatever to do with eau de nil carrying litters and the bare pink animals that toted them.

A metal grille was slid in front of Anita's cage and she was borne off to a shady corner to allow the soporific chocolate to do its work. We moved another carrying cage in front of the grille, removed the grille, slipped

open the door of cage number two and tried again. María had seen how our fiendish plan worked and it took an hour of wasted video tape, two camera batteries and an enormous amount of coaxing from Pável to get the bear to play.

Scene, therefore: one empty, scummy, mired and tick-infested cage. Two bear-filled carrying boxes. Five sweaty sunburnt Englishmen, assorted Peruvians and one very calm and efficient vet. Pável, I have decided, is just about the coolest human being on the planet. For the dismal salary of $250 a month he expends his years of training and specialisation on the largest and most disparate group of animals the world offers. He is an employee of INRENA, Peru's National Parks Authority, a loathsomely bureaucratic and corrupt organisation that must send him to despair, although he is fiercely loyal to them. He doesn't have so much as an air rifle to fire tranquillising darts (hence the absurd palaver with grilles and boxes) to call his own, yet his bailiwick covers six United Kingdoms.

Did I mention that he is INRENA's *only* vet? Over fifty parks, sanctuaries, protected areas, special breeding zones and wildlife refuges with precisely 1, figure ONE, veterinary surgeon employed to supervise them. Peru – Nature's most exuberant flourish and Man's most graceless failure. Yet an individual of his quality and dedication blunts the anger.

For the next quarter of an hour Pável set up his drugs,

hypodermics and other paraphernalia while the bears began to quieten. I wish some of my loonier anti-western medicine actor friends could have been there. All the implements of sterilisation, antibiosis, nutrition, pesticide and immunisation that the patience of science has accumulated over the years were laid out with methodical care. I don't think a crystal, a homeopathic pill and a session of aromatherapy would quite match up to that. There is more love in a sterile syringe than all the herbal teas in China. So there.

I took a photograph of Pável getting things ready before the bears were emboxulated.

Pável needed, amongst other things, to check diagnostic norms for these were his first ever bears of this age: they might be expected to live to 20 in captivity – in the wild, who knows? He also planned to take blood and samples of fur and ticks for laboratory analysis, which we were to pay for since INRENA refused to do so. Many times in the past he has paid for lab time out of his own underfilled pocket.

Once both bears were in their boxes we had to tip them up in turn, sending each outraged bear sliding to the grilled end, through which Pável could jab the anaesthetic. I don't know if such an operation *sounds* straightforward, but believe me in reality it isn't. Bears can stick their claws into anything and hang in defiance of gravity for as long as it takes for half a dozen humans to tire of supporting them. It was not achieved for another sweaty half-hour or so.

Pável was unhurried, tender and professional, neither minding the radio mike attached to him nor my inane questions. 'What's that?' 'Is her temperature normal?' and so on. He used a dextrose drip to carry minerals, vitamins, antibiotics, anti-tick drugs and so on into their bloodstream.

As he worked we filmed and recorded him while a team of pest controllers revved up their fogging engine and prepared their burner. The idea was to burn every bug in the cage while it was empty and then fog it with an insecticide that didn't harm bears. I hope it didn't harm humans either since we got a fair whiff of it and the pest men didn't wear masks.

Meanwhile Nick discovered from Juan on the phone that Lima Zoo had gone back on its word as far as the bears from Santiago are concerned and that more money was wanted. He was incandescent with rage. Our whole project was threatened. Santiago Zoo, where the bears from the circus were currently resting, had been reliable so far. They were ready for us but couldn't keep the bears for ever. They had to go to Lima. Everything was booked. Another problem arose. Anita and María have to stay put at Sr Suarez's hell-hole for at least three weeks. Pável had brought along a diet sheet for Suarez to follow. No one believed he would use our money for the fruit and vegetables the she-bears need. He would simply pocket it. Nick had given him

'Pável, I have decided, is just about the coolest human being on the planet.'

some on the recce and Pável said it was apparent they had not been well fed at all. If we gave Suarez the fruit he and his wife would eat it. Short of installing webcams there it's hard to know how we can guarantee their correct feeding. I suggested that Pocha may know someone in the immediate area who could be paid to come in and feed them personally:

$$Peru = Paradise \div El\ Niño + Earthquakes$$
$$+ Volcanoes + CORRUPTION$$

The last of all really, really ruining the equation.

By late afternoon the bears had been checked, injected and were recovered enough from the anaesthetic to be returned to their original cage. This involved reversing the original operation which was a little easier than it might have been since the bears were woozy and the sight that faced them this time was their old home, not a dark box. Anita was a little wonky on her pins.

We got home to the Casa de Pocha at about eight o'clock. A twelve-hour day and, what with the scorching sun and the particular stress that overcomes humans when confronted with large animals, we were exhausted. The same, I'm sure, went for the bears. We shall return tomorrow morning with fruit to see how they are getting along.

The Casa de P. is one of those places that has that special gift of always being further away, when you are driving to it at the end of a long day, than you remember. I must have started saying 'nearly there' to myself half an hour before we did finally arrive for dinner and, in my case, a session tap-tap-tapping at the keyboard.

I have been doing this diary not in my room which is too dark but in the 'charging room', an outhouse that has a wire that connects to the generator. John and Tim use it to charge the batteries their equipment uses and Nick to top up with current the phone he gives such a bashing every day. I have my Mac on a table. About my feet small chickens scuttle, bewildered by the light coming from the keyboard. In my hair moths the size of wrens fight it out for tenancy rights. It's peculiar, in Norfolk where I grew up and where I live when not poncing about in London, I have a great terror of moths and can't sleep if there's one in the room with me. I shout out loud if one so much as brushes my skin. Here they are larger, fatter and weirder than any of their English relations but I don't seem to mind them. Enough already. The hour of the cock is moving too swiftly forwards.

As Scarlett O'Hara likes to say, *Mañana es un otro diás*, or something like that. Ner-night.

———————————

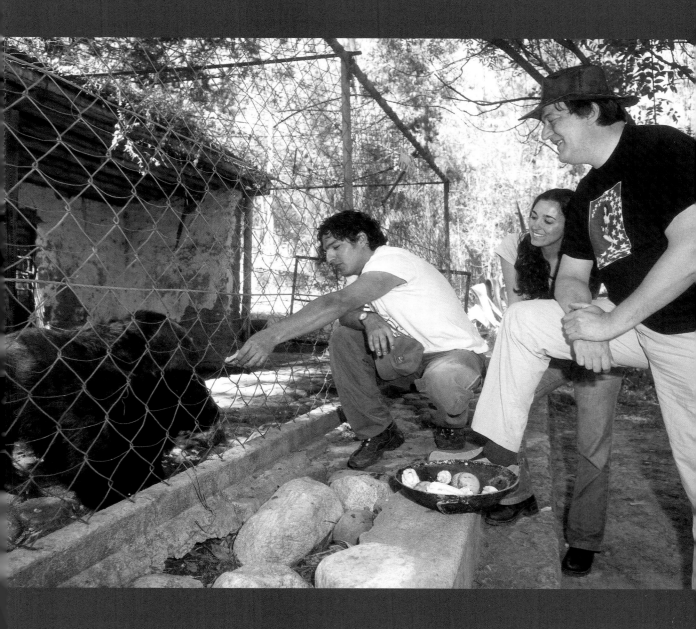

Wednesday 16 January, 2002
Miraflores Park Hotel, Lima

Back in Lima, hurrah and wassail. A bath, soft sheets, electricity, room service, laundry… I know I shouldn't care but God how I do.

I did one piece-to-camera in the field at the Casa de Pocha this morning showing where María and Anita will go and another pretending to point to the complete cage a few weeks later. They will insert footage of M and A frolicking there when a Peruvian crew has come to film it after we've long gone. Bit of a cheat but fair enough under the circumstances. On the nine-hour drive back to Lima we stopped off at the bears to feed them and for me to interview Pável on film. He had a sublime lack of TV sense and rattled away without giving Rocío a chance to interpret. His passion more than made up for this. Poor Rocío didn't have a prayer — apart from anything else she couldn't translate half the technical terms. I felt rather pleased at spotting 'alcohol etílico' go by and just grabbing it. It doesn't sound as like the English as it looks on the page.

The journey back was ghastly and bumpy and un-utterably tedious. Couldn't sleep, reading made me feel like vomiting and the batteries had gone on the Mac. More news of malversion, peculation and graft from

Juan on the phone to Nick. Now the people at Chiclayo have suddenly demanded six thousand US dollars to allow us to film. Since this is the only place we have a hope of seeing bears in the wild it's a hell of a blow. I was all for telling them that we'd changed our minds and now wanted to make a film about Peruvian corruption and the hypocritical greed which we have now discovered is the real problem hindering the bears' well-being. More bad news from Santiago airport concerning the papers and the bears there. It's all money. I can quite understand how the poor here, and my God there are millions of them, could legitimately say, 'You gringos care about the bears so much, you look after them. It's all we can do to eat.'

Heigh ho. I shall concentrate now on trying to put some of this diary on the web, or on Apple's server or somewhere handy.

———————————

Saturday 19 January, 2002
Santiago Sheraton, Chile
Pablo Neruda Suite

Yes, I'm afraid so. The Pablo Neruda Suite. Whether there is a Gabriele Mistral street or not, I have no idea, but Chile is proud of its Nobel laureate poets.

And what a suite this is. Nick Green has done me more than embarrassingly proud. I could have twelve to dinner in the dining room, cook it myself in the kitchen and play Twister with them all in the drawing room. The bedroom I would keep holy and wholly unto myself, since the Mac is there and the new iPod about which more later.

There is a difference of three hours *más o menos* between Chile and Peru and an incalculable difference in wealth, style, social grace and efficiency. I don't know what I had expected from Santiago, but it wasn't a city that, on the face of it at least, has more in common with Seville than with Lima. There is courtesy from the people and a universe more twinkle in the eye, confidence in the bearing and, actually, beauty. I am assured by Nick and Juan especially, who have an eye for these things, that the women are astonishingly lovely and I would agree from my position of ignorance. It is certainly true that the men are eye-poppingly attractive. It's confidence more than anything: assurance and poise and trust.

The fear that dominates Peru: fear of the police, fear of being ripped off, fear of being dismissed from work and the fear and shame of poverty become so much more apparent when you find yourself in a neighbouring country, more or less composed of the same stock but possessing less in the way of natural and human resources, yet which has good roads, a metro system, regular buses, cars that are safe and clean, modern, tree-lined avenues, well-preserved jewels of past architecture, and a people that smile, meet your eyes and banter with you. Does it make one believe in a tough dictatorship like that of Pinochet? Their President today is leftist but the foundation of consistent growth, debt-repayment and brimming export order-books was laid by the tin-pot *caudillo* who had Allende and Jara and thousands of others 'disappeared'. It's not for me to say that the price was worth paying, and they assure me on all sides, especially the Peruvians like Juan and Luz (she is our guide and helper here in Santiago), that there is great poverty in Chile and an ever widening disparity between rich and poor. It is not however, as Juan conceded, that the poor are getting poorer, it is that the rich are getting richer. But by Peruvian standards what I've seen in Santiago is universal prosperity.

In Lima every wall is covered with political slogans, in Santiago I saw none. In Lima there are no observable buses, just shabby and buckled minivans crammed with people, destinations hand painted on the outside. In Lima they lean on their horns half a second before the traffic lights turn green, in Santiago they wait until the lights are green and then either flick their lights or toot gently, as in Britain.

I think we all felt a little embarrassed about the pleasure we felt to be in a country that worked in all senses of the word. We filmed today, at Santiago Zoo: there were no problems with the staff, no demands for money, no blank stares or infuriating demands for paperwork, just cheery waves and amiable grins. They have shopping centres here. I went yesterday with Alan, the director, to one as large and as busy as Brent Cross or Bluewater. Today I visited one far ritzier. They had an Apple store called – two favourite words in one – Maconline, which sounds like a mail order wine merchants. They had an iPod and a Nikon Coolpix 995. I've spent most of this evening, while the others are out salsaing, setting them all up. Like a pig in Shiraz. I can't think of anything worse than sweating on a dance floor and I can't think of anything better than sitting alone in my room tweaking peripherals and wrestling with cable. Pathetic. I'm not always like that, it comes in cycles.

But we came here for bears, not for computer equipment or ill-informed political speculation. Some of the crew, most notably Alan Director and Tim Sound, have succumbed to Atahualpa's revenge, probably contracted

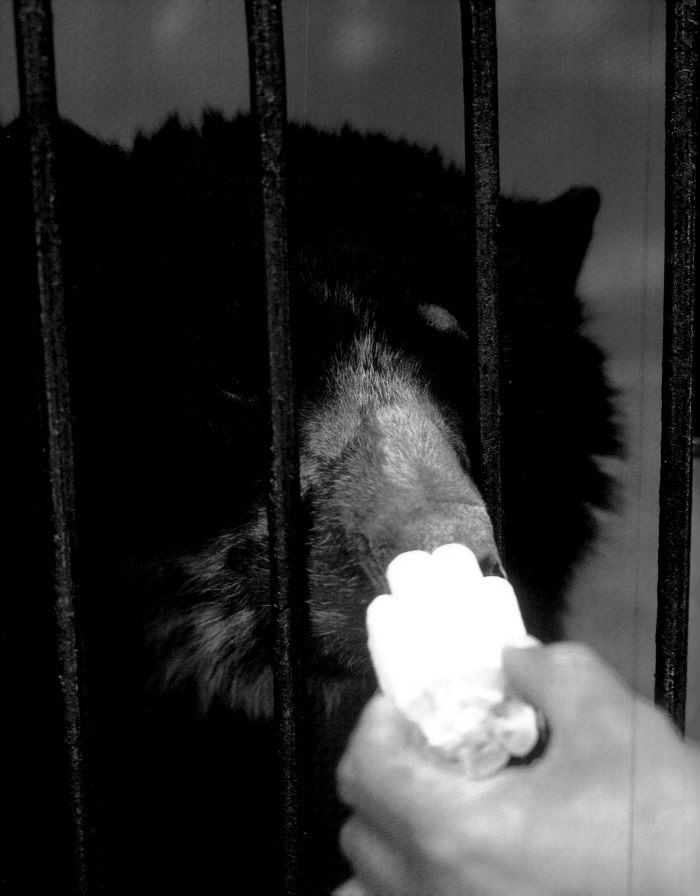

at the service station restaurant on the way back from Huaraz. I had a mess of seafood and rice there and my bowels are singing like a linnet. I should know better than to tempt providence like that, look what happened last week. My explosive episodes were nothing like poor T's and A's however.

Nonetheless we all met this morning at eight thirty and headed for San Cristóbal, the highest point in Santiago. I can't say the zoo is splendid, but those who work there are cheerful and the animals all seem well cared for physically. A large number, however, appeared neurotic and mentally unstable, circling and pacing and jumping and plucking in the way that bad actresses will insist upon doing when playing Ophelia in her mad scene.

The first animal we came across was a great shaggy grizzly bear. Its cage faced that of the spectacled cousins we had come to inspect and as we moved round we passed his back door, which had the tiniest inspection window − designed, I suppose, to stop him swiping at his keeper's face. As I passed he placed a nose and then an eye to this opening, as forlorn a symbol of the awful grimness of zoos as you could wish for.

I fully suppose that generations after us will look at our careless capacity to live at a time when animals live in prisons like this in much the same way that we look at our ancestors who happily stirred sugar into tea knowing that it had been picked by slaves.

The Spectacled Bears next door were just waking up, it being a Saturday morning and a day of rest. They are both male and have spent the greater part of their lives as an exhibit in a Chilean circus. The circus had bought them illegally from a poacher and put them on display in a caravan. Spectacled Bears aren't native to Chile so they can only have been smuggled. The circus was fined and the bears brought to Santiago Zoo. They don't have room so we have paid for a couple of flying cases and will transport them back to Peru on Monday. They will live out their lives in Lima Zoo, hardly a great improvement, but the cage will be roomier and since they have spent most of their lives in captivity I suppose they will adapt. The circus cannot have treated them as badly as Sr Suarez treated María and Anita; their size and the health of the coats bespeaks reasonable physical treatment. A nervous beating and bowing and stamping on the part of the second bear to emerge for breakfast shows the result of years of confinement however.

Nonetheless they seemed to breakfast quite happily.

The saner bear got stuck in early and the second spent a good two minutes producing a stream of urine of the longest duration I've ever seen proceed from a living creature. I don't know why I say that. It's not as if I've seen streams of urine emitting from robots.

A rather neat pile of poo was left behind also. Eventually bear two was done with his morning evacuations and lumbered to the feeding bowl. I know 'lumber' is a cliché when applied to the locomotion of bears, but no other word will do.

This is the first episode of cross-border co-operation between INRENA and SAG, the Chilean equivalent. Dr Gonzalo Gonzalez from Santiago Zoo, whom I interviewed on camera, seemed very pleased about this.

Anyway, we shot animals around the zoo. Vicuñas and tapirs and so on.

The most endearing sight was of a two-day-old giraffe. Dr Gonzalez let me into his little stable to do a p-to-c and take a snap.

Almost impossible to believe that such an elegant, self-possessed and gracefully tall creature had come from a womb two days earlier. He was a good foot higher than me and stared back in his shed with extremely talkative eyes. 'So this is life then, is it? Hm. I wonder. There's a stable with straw. There are people who make a lot of noise and shovel up my poo. There's a mother with highly pleasant udders and there's an enclosure outside with high fences. There's a blue ceiling there with a bright yellow ball that has twice dipped below the wall and made it all go dark. Now there's this tall person cooing at me and clicking to make me turn round. I wonder if I shall like this business of being alive. I seem to feel I should be galloping away from large cats in limitless plains. Heigh ho.' That's more or less an exact translation of what he said under his lashes as he gazed at me with a mild and good-natured curiosity.

I did a p-to-c in a cable car after this. It flies up to the top of the San Cristóbal hill where there is a huge sugar white statue of La Inmaculada Concepción, the kind of thing Hispanics like.

Shopped afterwards, while the crew did GVs of the city (General Views, the most wonderful words I ever hear, since they mean footage that doesn't have me in shot), and found the iPod. Thank God I've now got one that works. It seems mad to say one can't live without something that's only been on the market for two months but it's true, or as true as that sloppy formulation 'can't live without' ever is.

I bought a pipe too. Rob Fraser the stills photographer and his girlfriend Polly have been on at me about how it would suit me. I used to smoke one when I was a prep school teacher (since I was closer in age to the boys than to the rest of the staff I figured it would give me dignity: the only discernible result was the boys giving me the nickname The Towering Inferno) and have barely touched one since. I think I tried it during my first week at Cambridge: together with a tweed jacket I was going for that squinting into the sun look that Audenesque poets and university boffins adopted in the thirties. Disaster in the age of punk, of course. I sometimes puff on my own in Norfolk when writing, but have always felt that it's pretty hard not to look pompous with a pipe these days unless you're of a certain age. I have come to realise that I have been of that certain age for many years, so maybe now's the time. Given the amount I inhale I don't suppose it's much healthier, but maybe the smell is better. I seem to remember a footnote in the Ivy's menu forbidding their use. Being banned from the Ivy for improper use of pipes would hardly do. How could I ever look Ned Sherrin in the face again? Brrr, doesn't bear thinking about.

It's half past midnight already and surely time for sleep. We go to the beach tomorrow.

Tuesday 22 January, 2002
Miraflores Park Hotel, Lima

Bloody bloody hell. A whole day trying to rewrite the website with almost no success whatsoever. I won't get nerdy but it involves java rollovers and transparent backgrounds. Been screaming with anger and kicking the walls.

But this is wrong of me. We've blown out Chiclayo because of the six thousand dollars (up front) demanded by the people who run it (they claim it's some sort of sanctuary for bears, run in their charitable interest). A lot more serious than computer troubles. We did offer to pay that much so long as it was not in cash but sent in instalments that fitted the looking after of the bears, duly receipted and accounted for. They refused, which is a little more than fishy. If they truly care about the animals then they'll accept the money for their welfare legitimately and sensibly defrayed. Accountability is more than just pedantry when it comes to a charity. Absolutely maddening. We have a Canadian cameraman here who specialises in filming bears in the wild and now he has nothing to do, for this was an area of land where bears roamed free. Nick has been reworking the schedule like mad in an attempt to get things done. We are now off to Trujillo and Chan-Chán, a mud-brick adobe city. Then we'll come down to see how the Chilean bears are doing.

The bears were dozing in their sleeping quarters when we arrived. We were let into the cage – the sleeping quarters being separated by dropped iron grilles. By the time the vet arrived (late, of course) thirty-one people by my count (mostly Chilean press) had jammed themselves into the enclosure to watch. The number had grown to over fifty by the time the vet had pumped up his airgun and warned us not to stand in the line of fire. A good warning as it turned out since he managed to miss the first bear. A foot away and he discharged into the ground. The bears were getting a little disgruntled at the unwonted filling of their enclosure and the tension in the air. I dare say the darts puffing into the ground at their feet weren't helping either. They started to make noises like a cappuccino machine and do strange neurotic dances.

When they were both out they took about ten minutes to fall asleep. By the time the vet was sure they were unconscious the process of rolling each bear onto a cargo net and humping it down the hill to the flat-bed truck that contained our specially made travelling cages began.

Not dignified but it worked. We filmed, I did a few ps-to-c and then we followed the truck to Santiago airport, not in itself a triumph of modern film-making what with the truck thinking it was a race and our driver being the only courteous driver in South America and letting everyone in between the truck and our bus.

When we arrived at the airport a press conference had been set up and the SAG (Chilean wildlife organisation) and INRENA (Peruvian ditto of which I have spoken) sat next to each other and gave little speeches about how splendid this co-operation was. Official transport bills of bear-lading were then swapped and the pair were now officially Peruvian property again. We tried to get footage of them being loaded onto the plane but would have missed our own flight back to Lima.

I realised I had left my luggage back at the hotel, which wasn't a good start to the flight. Luz, our Santiago guide, was coming back on a later one so she was deputed to collect it from the hotel (whose fault it was I have to say in mitigation) and bring it later on.

Since then, because of Chiclayo's cancelling I've been stuck in my room swearing heavily at the computer. It's one of those days when I write over files by mistake and lose work. A screamingly irritating day. I might just go down and get drunk if I finish this in time to unload.

———————————

9

'Here is a city made of mud. The largest city on earth made of mud, certainly, but nonetheless a city that does exactly what it says on the tin.'

Wednesday 23 January, 2002
Miraflores Park Hotel, Lima

More delays, more demands for money, more struggles on the part of Juan and Nick to overcome new obstacles and more frustration at this damnably silly yet adorable country. Today we rose at four forty-five in the morning to catch a flight to Trujillo, Peru's third city, an elegant colonial town to the north.

Just next to it lie two impossibly peculiar sites, the mud city of Chan-Chán and the double pyramids of Huaca del Sol and Huaca de la Luna. The pyramids are also made of mud, and being imponderably old have suffered somewhat. The Huaca del Sol was once the largest man-made structure in the Western Hemisphere, but the *el niño* of the early eighties caused a great deal of it to rinse away. It was built by the Moche people who seem to have been a friendly, prosperous bunch who cleverly diverted rivers to make this part of northern Peru extremely fertile. So splendid was their diet that they had little else to do but make pots and textiles. They were taken over by the Chimú in 800 BC, give or take, who had the amusing idea of building an enormous city out of mud.

Very difficult to know what to say on camera. 'Here is a city made of mud. The largest city on earth made of mud, certainly, but nonetheless a city that does exactly what it says on the tin.'

I think we all got a little hysterical under a very searing sun wandering about a city made of mud. I moved from one mud area to another while John filmed. There were corridors of mud, squares of mud and wine bins made of mud (though our archaeologist guide Jesús claimed they were purely decorative: if this is true then the Chimú missed a trick).

The idea next was to visit the Huaca de la Luna and the Huaca del Sol. We took one look and saw that these eroded pyramids were made ... of mud. The patience of the BBC viewer is great but not, I think, so monumental as to endure a documentary that gives them more than one construction made of mud. We passed on the Huacas and headed for the seaside town of Huanchaco to a restaurant called Big Ben whose oddities merit close attention.

There is one thing I haven't discussed and that is Peruvian food. It is generally excellent (when not playing host to explosive enteric bugs, that is). On the coast, as you might expect, there is seafood of the very highest quality. Octopus, squid, scallop and a white fish called *corvina* that the dictionary gives as sea bass, but which seems to have little in common with its Atlantic or Mediterranean cousin, are often marinated raw in lemon juice and onions in the form of a *cebiche*. These are often served with corn of enormous nibs that put the Jolly Green Giant to shame, yellow sweet potato, chilli and yuca, all Peruvian delicacies. A drink that comes second to pisco in the National Drink of Peru League is called *Algarrobina* (a carob-based liqueur which tastes like a Bailey's Irish cream that has been left out in the sun). The restaurant where I enjoyed all this, Big Ben, is a touristic institution par excellence and boasts as splendid a brochure as you can imagine.

Beware all fish restaurants above whose menu grins a cartoon fish dressed in waiter's clothes, clutching a knife and fork and smacking its lips, someone probably once said. The owners of Big Ben do boast one possession that marks them out from the common run of Peruvian restaurants however, an English dictionary. Perhaps this is a mistake: if instead of lashing out on a Harrap's pocket Spanish-English they had called up a friend who spoke English they might not have had such a tricky time with their brochure.

> *Our Restaurant has several atmospheres. All with view to the sea, inviting them to choose between their warm living rooms and their wide terrace to assist their family lunches, of business agazajos, etc.*

My dictionary doesn't have 'agazajo' either, so I can't help you there.

> *Discovers with us the delights that offers our sea, in a*

*varied selection of plates; with the flavour, the quality
and the good pleasure that it always characterizes us.*

Absolutely. We get the idea: the following paragraph
however is more obscure.

*On behalf of a group of local entrepreneurs decided to
bring to him/her/you prosperity to this people, being
strengthened by offering to him/her/you to the visitor
the quality of services and hospitality that is
deserved… You/them we give the Welcome!*

My word processor's extensive grammar checker has
just exploded.

*Huanchaco, legendary fisherman cove nailed in the
northern department of The Freedom, it was the port
that supplied to the nearby city of Chan Chan
erected by the mythical Prince Takaynamo 'Come of
the other side of the Sun' to disembark in our beaches
makes 800 years, establishing the first dynasty of the
Great Empire Chimú.*

Maybe a legendary prince who built a city out of mud
deserves no better.

*This beautiful resort during all year round enjoys a
privileged climate and an animate Tourist Calendar.*

In winter particularly is converted into a backwater of peace where the visitor can enjoy spectacle the ditches in rafts Totora, table championships, an assorted gastronomy, modern hotel facilities and a brilliant sun; not to no avail the Tourism Ministry has qualified it as 'National Tourist Center'.

After we had gorged ourselves on the several atmospheres and the varied selection of plates we drove to Trujillo where dozens of shoe-shiners awaited us. It was as if a legend existed in Trujillo that one day a coach filled with pink gringos would arrive. Almost every man, woman and child had been waiting since their birth for this prophecy to be realised. On the 23rd of January 2002 it was. The moment we stepped from the coach we were surrounded by the faithful. That I was wearing suede boots made no difference: the Ones Who Were Written Of had arrived and their boots must be polished and their dollars extracted or the gods would punish them: perhaps with another city made of mud.

Alan was swept up by a child slightly smaller than his boots. Nick seemed to enjoy the attention and John, professional as ever, spotted a progression of street lamps down the street that pleased his cameraman's eye.

A small girl was angry at finding us too late: perhaps her particular sect believed that when we arrived it would be around the corner in another street.

The city abounds in fine examples of vice-regal colonial architecture, unlike poor Lima which has been modernised into gehenna.

The main square, the Plaza Mayor, is very grand. Trujillo is the capital of the department La Libertad (which Big Ben's brochure so kindly translated for us as The Freedom) and there is a giant statue representing Liberty triumphing over her enemies, the writhing figures of Slavery, Poverty, Imperialism, People Who Won't Pay More Than Five Dollars To Have Their Shoes Ruined and so on. Once Trujillo had given up its glories to digital tape we returned to the airport and hung around for an hour or so before catching the flight back to Lima.

Thursday 24 January, 2002
Miraflores Park Hotel, Lima

Today we went to Lima Zoo to inspect the Chileno bears. They seemed fairly fit. A splendid girl called Claudia who had helped us for the Paddington film is now a big Peruvian TV star, presenting a Sunday morning political programme à la *Frost On Sunday*. She won Anti-Corruption Journalist of the Year recently and the reach of her programme makes her a powerful ally. She accompanied us to the zoo to film us filming bears for a piece on her show which will be dedicated to the subject of our programme.

The bears, called with an alarming lack of originality Yogi and Boo-Boo (alarming because it seems that only American TV cartoons penetrate the culture here), are in quarantine sharing space with monkeys, a beautiful but wicked-looking ocelot, snakes, macaques and baboons-stroke-gibbons-never-been-quite-sure-of-difference.

The morning had begun with another crisis, this time from INRENA again who had decided that we could not move any bears anywhere without them inspecting the premises to which they were going to be moved: this would take three months minimum. In other words the entire film would be ruined, the bears would all stay in zoos and cages and nothing would be done. A part of me had to admire this manoeuvre, since INRENA would always be able to say that their motive was ensuring the very best care for the animals. Nick's face was greyer that morning than I've ever seen it.

By the time we returned from the zoo to the hotel everything, following furious phone conversations and meetings between Juan and everyone influential he knows in Lima, the problem seemed to have resolved itself. It's as if they're testing the strength of our coronary systems.

I had dinner this evening with Jim and Shirley Sherwood and their son Simon. The Sherwoods are the owners of the Orient Express Group which includes this hotel as well as the Hotel Monasterio in Cusco, the Machu Picchu Sanctuary Lodge, a boat on Lake Titicaca and the rail line from Lima to Cusco (featured in the Paddington film). Their enterprise is enormous around the world though they manage to visit everything once a year: there are worse lives I suppose.

11

'One of the greatest and most extraordinary sights that Peru can offer can be found halfway down the coast, in the middle of the driest desert in the world.'

Friday 25 January, 2002
Miraflores Park Hotel, Lima

One of the greatest and most extraordinary sights that Peru can offer can be found halfway down the coast, in the middle of the driest desert in the world. The desert strip runs between the Pacific and the Andes: something to do with the Humboldt current and the weather systems created by the mountains that dry up the land between the mountains and the sea. Here there has been no significant rainfall since the last Ice Age. Round about 400 BC the Nasca people who inhabited this fierce region began to do something very peculiar indeed.

There is a plateau, or *pampa* that rises five hundred metres above the rest of the desert and on the lifeless surface of this *pampa* the Nasca began to etch drawings and lines. The scale of them is remarkable and their use, purpose and reason has been a matter of fierce conjecture since they were properly discovered in modern times round about seventy years ago. A German mathematician named Maria Reiche devoted fifty years of her life to uncovering the animals depicted on the *pampa* and devising theories to explain the phenomena.

The most preposterous and least believable theory is, unfortunately, the best known. A fraudulent and absurd book called *Chariots of the Gods*? came out in the nineteen seventies by one Erich von Daniken in which he claimed that the Nasca Lines (*inter alia*) were proof of an extra-terrestrial presence in South America fifteen hundred years ago. The trapezoidal lines, he claimed, were landing-strips left there should these aliens wish one day to return. It boggles the imagination that anyone could believe such nonsense. If they were capable of interplanetary transport and could land there in the first place why would they need to draw crude landing strips to be able to do it again?

Other, less wacko explanations involve the inevitable 'stellar calendar' theory. Pre-Christian man seems to have been unable to build anything without us interpreting it as some kind of 'cosmic timepiece'. Some of the lines, according to Maria Reiche, point to where the sun would have risen at that time during the winter solstice. Since 'that time' spans a period of about a thousand years and there are so many lines going in so many different directions on the *pampa*, this theory too seems a little hard to swallow.

The problem with unexplained phenomena is that they allow all the loonies in. Chesterton said that the trouble with people who stop believing in God is not that they believe nothing, it's that they believe *anything*. So let it be with the Nasca Lines. Simply because there is not yet a rational explanation does not mean that any irrational one will do.

Perhaps the most believable, or perhaps least unbeliev-able is that there was a terrible drought round about AD 550 and that the lines are desperate pleas from the Nasca to encourage the water to flow from the moun-tains. Each year the rainy season in the Andes causes water to stream down past the *pampa* to the sea and it was on this that they relied (and still do) for their food. The trapezoids and lines were etched it seems round about this time, the animal shapes having been done in earlier perhaps more exuberant times (not unlike our own white horses and Cerne Abbas man). This drought of AD 550 had a colossal effect on the whole continent, right up to the Aztec areas of Central America where whole cities were abandoned, so this theory has some tenability.

One of the effects of Daniken's book was to cause all manner of hippies and freaks to visit the Nasca Lines in the seventies and drive all round them on jeeps and bikes: the surface is so dry that everything remains, for ever, like the lines themselves. Such gross vandalism is now forbidden and no one is allowed on the surface of the *pampa*.

We drove down this morning in a bus, having risen at 3.30 a.m., so as to be there in time for the earliest light. The best way to see the lines properly is from the air. Not the *only* way as some believe (the animals are visible clearly from surrounding hillocks) but certainly the best. If you fly over at midday the air currents make

'Pre-Christian man seems to have been unable to build anything without us interpreting it as some kind of "cosmic timepiece".'

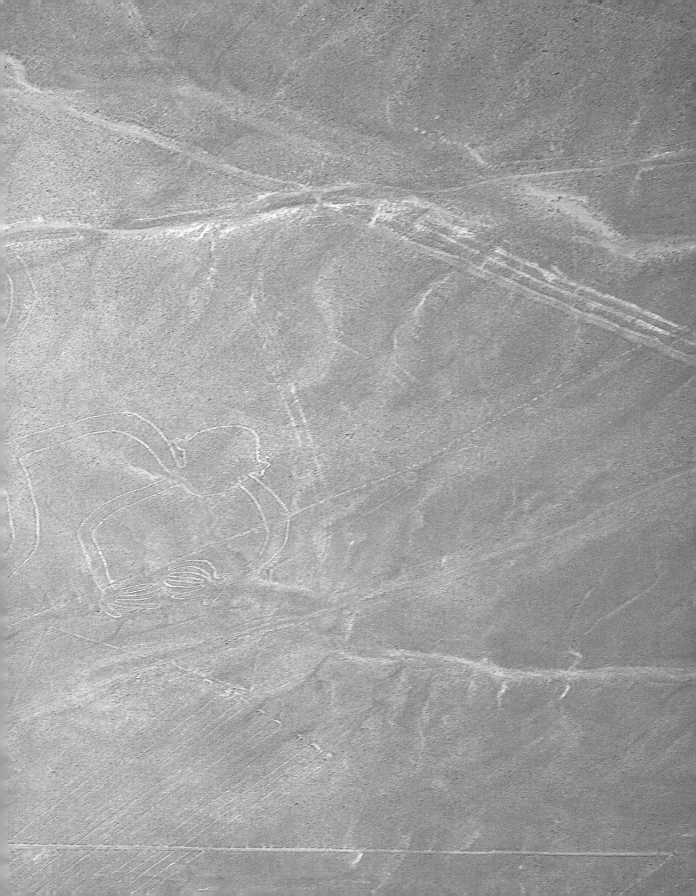

it too bumpy to film, so we had to get there for nine o'clock.

There is a kind of visitors' centre ten or twelve miles from the *pampa* with a cafeteria, a museum and a (genuine) landing strip.

The plane was a Cessna Grand Caravan and John and I got on last so that he could shoot out the window from my point of view and then film me gawping at the lines. The first animal one comes across is called, in irritating deference to Daniken, The Astronaut, on account of an apparent helmet.

The next to be visible was the Hummingbird, my favourite. There is a monkey, perhaps second favourite. A spider is also clearly visible. As are a pair of human hands, close by to the observation post or 'mirador' that Reiche had constructed.

By the time we got back to Lima it was early evening and I fell asleep that night looking forward to two days off and dreaming of weird lines vanishing into space. Terrestrial space that is, terrestrial space …

———————————

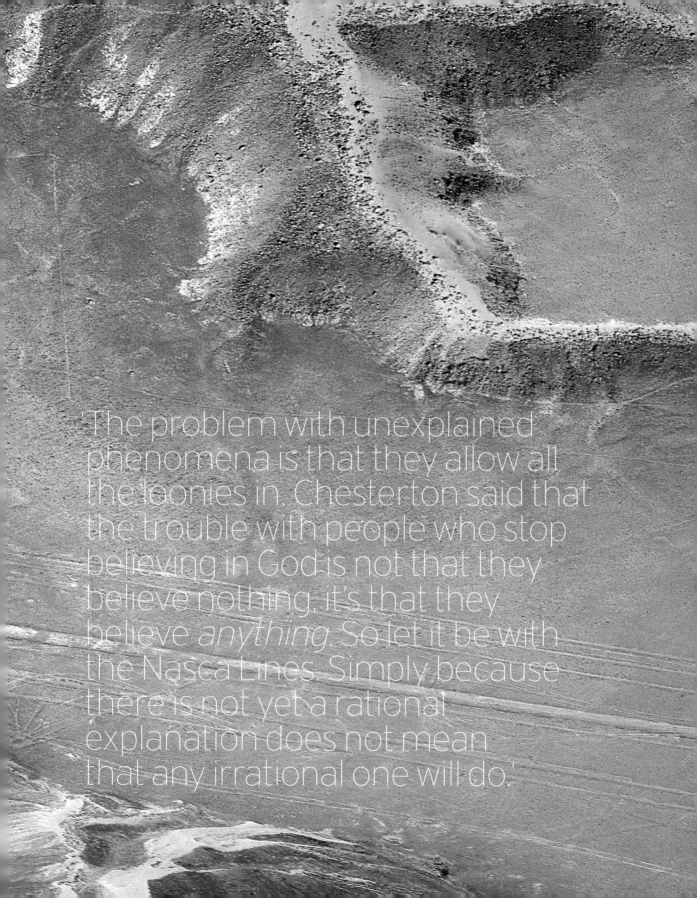

'The problem with unexplained phenomena is that they allow all the loonies in. Chesterton said that the trouble with people who stop believing in God is not that they believe nothing, it's that they believe *anything*. So let it be with the Nasca Lines. Simply because there is not yet a rational explanation does not mean that any irrational one will do.'

Saturday/Sunday 26/27 January, 2002
Miraflores Park Hotel, Lima

'Days off. Relaxing. Mike Matson from Apple arrived. He is to set up the website, bear cams and so forth. Clearly knows his stuff. A Quicktime expert. The site he built in Botswana is magnificent. Rest of weekend spent eating too much. More of that below.'

Monday 28 January, 2002
Miraflores Park Hotel, Lima

Oh God. It's back. The exploding stomach. It began on Sunday night. I was awake every twenty minutes, hosing down into the bowl. Then the vomiting followed. Fourteen hours of hell. Shall I tell you about the lack of control and the bed linen? I shall spare you that. You've been kind enough to follow me thus far and do not deserve to be taken into such a dark and depraved world.

I was due to interview the First Lady, wife of President Toledo, in her office this afternoon at five o'clock. Nick rang anxiously every hour or so to see if I was capable. It seemed to me that we could not let this opportunity pass: it would be invaluable for the sake of our Bear Foundation to have her on our side.

At the appointed time I came down, in my suit (as constructed by the Smelliest Tailor in Peru – I swear it still stinks) and my shoes (as sent from Norwich) and fell into the bus.

I remember almost nothing of the interview that followed: the FL spoke in Spanish, the British Ambassador by my side interpreted and joined in ably. I nodded and gulped and wittered. I gave the FL a video copy of the original Paddington programme and a large

Paddington Bear, she gave me a most charming cigar box. I staggered out and we drove back to the hotel where I was decanted to my bedroom where I received a visit from the most Charming Doctor in Peru, Doctor Pablo Boza, who for some reason reminded me of my grandfather. His English was excellent and he seemed to find my condition both sad and faintly amusing, which is just the encouragement one needs. You don't feel you've wasted his time, but you also feel that you aren't going to die. Both feelings are necessary for the sensitive patient. A couple of injections to stop the vomiting and allow ingress of pills, a life's supply of Gatorade and admonitions as to diet for the next few days. No alcohol till the weekend. No dairy produce.

It was realised that I was not going to be fit to travel tomorrow, Tuesday, when we were due to fly to Cusco and drive out in four-wheel-drive vehicles to the jungle. So Tuesday is another day off and the whole schedule will leak over to another day. I feel guilty about this, but there's nothing I can honestly do.

———————————

Tuesday January 29, 2002
Miraflores Park Hotel, Lima

Feeling a little better. May be able to eat some time today. The sun is shining outside and I am sitting here trying to update the websites.

Wednesday 30 January, 2002
Miraflores Park Hotel, Lima

I am in the peculiar position of actually being filmed as I write this: I don't know if it'll make the final cut of the film, but John and the others are on the balcony above, filming me as I mistype and try to look soigné and efficient. We shan't travel now until tomorrow, which is essentially my fault for being ill.

13

'Jungle!
I am in the jungle.
I am Fry of the jungle.'

Thursday 31 January, 2002
Inkaterra Lodge, Tambopata, la Selva del sur

Jungle! I am in the jungle. I am Fry of the jungle. Frankly my fingertips are too slippery to type this, and sweat could well drop from my brow or nose through the keyboard and short the computer out, but I shall press on nonetheless.

It is one of Peru's limitless joys that thirty minutes' flight from Cusco, the ancient Incan capital high, high, high up in the Andes, you can be transported to a landscape, an atmosphere, a world so different that it would be astonishing if it took six hours by Concorde. In less than two hours flying time one passes from the Pacific Ocean over the driest desert in the world, the second highest mountain range in the world to touch down in the interior of the greatest tropical rain forest in the world.

We arose at six-ish and flew from Lima to Cusco, staying twenty minutes on the apron while Mike Matson deplaned to start his webcam stuff. From Cusco to Puerto Maldonado, a lazy, seedy place that lies at the confluence of the Madre de Dios and Tambopata rivers, giving it the deliciously disreputable air of a Sidney Greenstreet or Wallace Beery location. You feel that people come here to trade in smuggled emeralds, or escape the clutches of the cartel ... rickshaws pulled by boys on Chinese-assembled Honda 125s buzz like hornets between the airport and the landing stage where the two rivers turn into one. What's that dialogue in the opening scene of *Casablanca*? 'Vultures, vultures everywhere ...' the man tells the British tourists as he expertly picks their pockets. That kind of place. 'Careful, Señor Fry! Your life won't be worth a moment's purchase if they know you have the map...' I half expected someone to whisper in my ear.

A thatched riverboat was waiting to take us to the Incaterra Lodge, another place run by the indomitable Joe Koechlin, whose Pueblo Hotel in Aguas Calientes houses the bear we found in the Paddington programme. More of the Pueblo and the great Joe Koechlin later.

The Madre de Dios area, including the Manu reserve and the Tambopata is part of the Amazon basin – though the Amazon river itself is hundreds and hundreds of miles north. All land east of the Andes tilts gently down eastwards, so rivers must flow to the Atlantic even if, as is the case here, it involves a journey of some 6,000 kilometres from raindrop to sea – a hundred times longer than it would take for them to empty into the Pacific. That's gravity for you. They won't flow up the Andes. Can't be done.

The moment you're in jungle you know it ... actually

let's start being sensible here. Jungle is a meaningless word. Kipling gave it to us, but it means in its own Indian 'what's out there: the exterior: nature' something like that. The technical term for where I am today is, so they tell me, 'subtropical moist forest'. The Peruvians call it 'la Selva del sur' the southern jungle. In theory it's slightly less wet than your full-on rain forest, though we're here in January at the height of the rainy season and the river is a great mud-red swollen torrent, wider than the Thames at any point I've ever seen it and busy with logs and river rubbish. At first I had thought with a leap of disbelief in my gut that there was a huge logging operation going on, so many tree corpses seemed to be floating with us downstream. Of course it is just that; when the rain comes it takes with it all the debris of the jungle floor. In the dry season the jungle floor includes much of what is now river.

So then: the moment you're in subtropical moist forest you know it. That's silly. We'll stick to jungle. The smell is green and sappy at the top, hotly metallic in the middle and warm vanilla cream in the bass. It's one of those 'I've been here before in another life' places: the other life being a mixture of Henty, Kipling, Biggles, Clark Gable, Tarzan, *Emerald Forest*, *Fitzcarraldo*, *The Mission* and who knows what in between. Scooby Doo and Conrad, I suppose. Not to mention a thousand BBC wildlife programmes.

The noise is extraordinary. More of that when we

come to the night time.

The Inkaterra is half an hour's Honda-putt downriver of Puerto Maldonado, a dream of thatched huts on the bank of the Madre de Dios. I tottered as ungracefully as only I know how off the gangplank and onto the steps that lead up to the lodge. The pathway is made of raised slices of logs set into the ground six inches proud in case of floods and curves gracefully towards the main building, a kind of beehive with a huge round roof which serves as dining room, bar reception, lounge and general meeting place. We were welcomed outside by drinks wrapped in palm leaves, a jungle fruit cordial of some kind, and by the staff and a curry powder green monkey that was very interested indeed in the fruit drink. Monkeys, I think, are animals of which one can tire very quickly on a social level. Entertaining as they at first appear and comely as they unquestionably remain, in fur and form, there is about their features a malevolent glare, a greed and a message of selfishness that puts one in mind of very dreadfully spoilt infants. There is a message in their faces that admits no possibility of affection on their part. They get attached to people, and scratch those who come close to their favourites, but you always sense that it comes from egotism not devotion. In *our* world this is: that's why they make appalling pets. In their own world they are magnificent. While this yallery-greenery primate made a mess of the drinks a pair of magnificent macaws looked down from the trees. I suppose if you run a lodge in the middle of the jungle tame parrots and monkeys are more or less de rigueur. It worked on me: and to call them tame was to insult them. They were wild but chose to live hard by the lodge. They were joined later by a dazzling toucan, but at a time when it was too late to photograph without flashing him out of the tree in shock.

Everything at the lodge is simple and wooden. Except the phone lines and air conditioning, which don't exist. The rooms are open thatched huts with a porch where two inviting hammocks invite you to spend the hot afternoon dozing and dreaming. Inside a couple of beds encased in anti-mosquito netting and a couple of wash basins scooped from a great trunk of wood. Two tilley lamps are offered for light at night.

We lunched quickly and returned to the river for a cruise up to a place where we could go inland. I found myself childishly delighted by being able to pluck a cacao berry from a tree, knock it open on the trunk and suck the beans. How man ever thought you could get from the viscous mess inside this yellow fruit to a bar of chocolate absolutely beats me. A little further inland we found a little lagoon where the skeleton of an old paddle steamer sat with water up to its middle. It was named *Fitzcarrald* in honour of the great and obsessional rubber-baron Fitzcarrald immortalised in the Herzog movie. I did a brief p-to-c about this and we tottered back to the bank for some more cruising. Back

'The smell is green and sappy at the top, hotly metallic in the middle and warm vanilla cream in the bass.'

at the lodge we met a huge group of American eco-students who have been here for three weeks earnestly attending classes and being washed under the arms and far too American to be bitten by mosquitoes. No such luck for us. No matter how much you Deet yourself with repellent some part of you will be chewed to buggery.

As soon as I stepped into the boat some message was posted in the insect world to the effect that the equivalent of the Ivy Restaurant had just opened in Tambopata and that it was large and pink and open twenty-four hours a day. The most popular feasting area, the David and Elton table if you like, is the little vein that throbs just forward of the temple. They've barely time to sweep away the spilt blood and reset the cutlery before the next party of diners is swooping down and asking for everything on the menu. Second favourite, Posh and Becks, is the shin. It's nice to be loved I suppose even if the way they show it is to leave you with the complexion of an adolescent burger-flipper. They say there is no malaria in this part of South America so that's something.

For dinner at the lodge we had chicken prepared in a remarkable manner. Pieces of meat are pushed, together with peppers, tomato, onion and a touch of the obligatory *ají* pepper, down a tube of bamboo, wrapped in palm leaf and steamed. It is plopped out of the bamboo onto a bed of rice. More tender and delicious than any chicken I have ever tasted.

As I walked along the glazed wooden corridor that separates the beehive from the huts I could tell from the noise around me that sleep was not going to be easy.

By oil-lamp light I sprayed myself and the mosquito netting with about a gallon of anti-mozzie juice and climbed into bed, carefully tucking the net back under the mattress. A moth about the size and weight of the Penguin Classics edition of *Don Quixote* flapped in and started circling the tilley lamp. First mistake. Swearing lightly, I pushed myself out of the netting and took the lamp out onto the porch. Creatures of the night, being dark and stupid, are attracted to the light. THEN WHY THE HELL DON'T THEY COME OUT DURING THE DAY?

Never mind: like a groom flicking confetti from his hair on the honeymoon night, I brushed a dozen assorted horrors of the insect world from my sweaty locks and repeated the mozzie netting business.

I think the noise had only dimly been on my mind before this point. I had been concentrating too much on avoiding cockroaches underfoot and folding clothes away high and out of tarantula reach (yes there really are tarantulas here) for the sound to make much of an impression. Now that I was alone and nudely panting in my mosquito tent crushed by the deep black of the night, the astonishing sounds of the night began to make themselves known to me.

In the manner of Cole Porter's 'Now You Has Jazz': the sounds of the jungle night are composed thus: first you take a snare drum a thousand feet in diameter and upon it you place a million steel wing-nuts. You put the whole contrivance on a giant pulsing vibrator of some kind. This is your basic background, a kind of rhythmic snare buzzing, but on a titanic scale. Cicadas I suppose, but who can tell? I can't honestly believe the scraping of a few little insect legs could possibly cause so enormous and all-encompassing a sound. It is all around you and never lets up for one second. At six o'clock, the man from the seventies dinner-party who always set the table on a roar with his trimphone impression will butt in from time to time with his entertaining chirrup. Fourteen or fifteen people closer to you, sometimes alarmingly close, idly run the back of their thumbnails along a comb for no reason. A whoop appears out of nowhere and, once started, is repeated with same insistent monotony as the 'Barmy Army!' chant of the England cricket groupies. Some one or thing starts to say 'Frint' and won't stop. Another one or thing, possibly related to the trimphone impersonator, suddenly starts doing a water droplet impression: a kind of echoey 'prip'. If there isn't already a species of bird or possibly frog called The Bren Gun, then I've discovered one, for that starts up too, rat-tat-tatting at first to the left and then to the right of you. It's all getting a little worrying.

But, as the sweat spirals around your neck and you feel

your pupils dilate enough to see, or imagine that they see, quite horrid shapes and sights at the window, the brain slowly accustoms itself to this great screen of sound: for it is rhythmic and sleep seems a possibility. That's when a blood-curdling scream as of a young girl having her hair pulled by an ogre suddenly explodes so close to you that you leap from your bed shouting in fear.

What the hell was that?

It must be in the room with you. Even if it's only a monkey or a lorikeet it's too much, far too much to bear. You shout louder and smack your sodden pillow in a way that wouldn't frighten a dove, but what else can you do? Run from your room into the night?

Somehow you settle again. And this time a creature speaks, calmly and with great assurance.

'Parsimony.'

You hear it quite clearly and now you know you have gone mad. Parsimony? Why would a jungle creature speak English? And if he did why would he say 'parsimony'? It makes no sense. No sense at all. But it was so clear and so nakedly forthright that the ghost of the word still seems to stand out in the night like the aural equivalent of a retinal after-image.

You're miles from mummy and there are screaming things and buzzing things and flapping things and things that say 'parsimony'. And, now – dear God – and now there's something scratching at the door.

It's stopped scratching and now it's slithering round the corner.

There's only one thing to do. Why didn't you think of it before?

You get out of your bed once more, stamping hard on the ground and whistling to show the whole alien hor–rible jungle that you don't care a bit, and you reach into your sponge bag pulling out twice the recommended dose of Zopiclone sleeping tablets.

They take about twenty minutes to kick in. Twenty minutes of howling and buzzing and plucking and scratching and screeching and laughing and repeated assurances of parsimony but in the end you're in a place where you don't care what threatens or mocks or tor–ments or bites you, nor what might slither or crawl over you and when you wake up it's a shining day full of bright parrots and green fronds and dappled light and wonderful, miraculous jungle smells that fill you with a heavenly and unabashed joy.

———————

14

'The journey off the river into a kind of jungle Venice is way beyond my powers of description. I say a kind of jungle Venice because the difference between a waterway, which a river is, and pure jungle which just happens to be flooded enough to allow a boat to pass through it is enormous.'

Friday 1 February, 2002
Incaterra Lodge, Tambopata, la Selva del sur

We wanted to catch the sunrise so it was an early, early call that jerked me from Zopiclone torpor into the delights of a jungle morning. We took the boat to a *cocha*, the local name for one of the many ox-bow lakes that the rivers have left in their ancient meanders over time. They are marvellously beautiful and John was in danger of running out of tape I think. We had only brought a certain amount from Lima and it has to last us till Monday evening. The journey off the river into a kind of jungle Venice is way beyond my powers of description. I say a kind of jungle Venice because the difference between a waterway, which a river is, and pure jungle which just happens to be flooded enough to allow a boat to pass through it is enormous. A river, in the end, is a river, and the banks you look at are all much the same. You want to be *in* there, but human passage through the jungle really does require the machete of schoolboy fiction (and Colombian crime-lord fact). But gliding through jungle, passing trees that are half submerged and glimpsing the canopy above with its vultures, hawks, quetzal birds, parakeets and monkeys, that is a different thing altogether. And then suddenly to find yourself in a huge curved lake, its own astounding ecosystem … well, you are Professor Challenger and Blashford–Snell and Colonel Fawcett all in one.

The boat dropped us at one end of the lake where a real path does exist offering a healthy hour's walk back to the river bank where we would be picked up. The walk forward featured the sight of miles and miles of ants, each one carrying a leaf on its back. There are more ants in the jungle – well, no one knows how many there are. Any square yard contains more than you could ever count. Their organised power makes them, our guide José Luis told me, the most fearsome and powerful predator in the jungle. On earth. One of the beauties of the jungle is the flowers of course, most especially the Heliconias, a specimen of the most famous of which, the passion–flower, was plucked for me by José Luis. (I say this in case you might think I had killed so beautiful a thing myself.) José Luis was born around here and loves and knows and cares about the jungle as much as anyone alive and if he thinks it's okay to pick a flower, then it must be. They're not rare here after all – it's like plucking a daisy to him. The fact that it'll cost you eighty quid in London is not the point really.

By the time we got to the river bank and had waited half an hour to be picked up we were ready for lunch and a siesta. I had not been wrong about those ham-mocks. I do not exaggerate when I say that I cannot remember a deeper or more fulfilling pleasure than the sleep I had this afternoon, the more benevolent daytime chatter of the jungle in my ears, my body suspended in a hammock swinging gently each time I shifted a happily weary limb.

Nick woke me at about four to start some filming, a silly but unavoidable scene of me shaving with a cut-throat razor in front of a hanging wooden frame mirror … if you're in the jungle you've got to do that really, haven't you?

At night we went out to look for black Caymans, the alligator-like creatures that come out to play in the dark. It was a long journey up river and we only glimpsed two for long enough to film, plus many shining eyes, but on the return journey to the lodge I lay on my back and feasted on the stars. I didn't mention this in my obsession with the horrors of the night, but one of the greatest miracles of this part of the world is the night sky. Firstly, of course, there is no light pollution from urban centres anywhere within three hundred miles, which helps enormously, but secondly the night sky here is, even in Lima, astounding. In the jungle it is breathtaking. The Milky Way has always been a phrase (and a sweet that you can eat between meals without ruining your appetite) to me, but in Peru you understand its name – a great opalescent smeary ribbon across the sky, as clear as anything. When I was here last I disgraced myself by looking up the first night in Peru and exclaiming, 'What the hell's that?' I have to admit, quite honestly that I'd never seen it in British skies. I have since, because I've looked and looked hard. Here you don't have to.

When the sun sets a planet appears, ping! right above you. Venus I suppose. Five minutes later Mars emerges close by, as red as red. Then another planet and then, within a few moments, the sky has turned the deep violet colour I once believed was an invention of romantic fiction and a great pulsing net of stars seems to have been laid open all at once. There is no area where stars are not. It's of a piece with the whole efflorescent, bulging and riotous abundance and generosity of this part of the world. I don't know much more than the obvious constellations in the northern hemisphere and I wished I had Brian May or Patrick Moore beside me to point out each strange new pattern.

Certain experiences enforce with a Homer Simpson 'Doh!' the obvious truth of cliché. The jungle is one such. Violet skies, I have already mentioned. A tropical night is another. How many song lyrics or prose pas-sages have spoken of tropical nights. You don't connect until you're in the middle of one and then you find yourself hearing the phrase as if for the first time.

I am ready for the Dark Side of the tropical night and have swallowed the sleeping pills before undressing and starting on this entry which I shall now finish as I'm dopey. And the battery's going. No power here. Except the real power. Which is useless for Apple Macs.

'Creatures of the night,
being dark and stupid,
are attracted to the light.
THEN WHY THE HELL
DON'T THEY COME OUT
DURING THE DAY?'

Saturday 2 February, 2002
Hotel Monasterio, Cusco

Another beautiful jewel in the crown of the Orient Express Group, this hotel is an old sixteenth-century Spanish monastery wonderfully reinvented as a hotel in this, the old Incan capital city of Cusco, almost three miles up in the Andes. I'm a little breathless and headachy from the *soroche*, as they call altitude sickness here. It's only fifty minutes from the jungle, but a whole other world. I keep going on about that, but it's still hard to get used to. Damn, I wish I'd paid more attention to geography at school. After the incredible humid heat of la Selva del sur, Cusco seems freezing. For one thing the air, as well as being thin, is dry and that makes the difference.

  We left early so as to get some footage of me arriving, leaving, arriving leaving and arriving and leaving Puerto Maldonado. Alan Director then thought it would be amusing if I went to the airport by Honda-powered rickshaw while they filmed me from the comfort of the back of the open bus. I bounced along trying not to blink too much from the dust or retch too much from the oily smoke – the benevolent air of the English milord favouring the locals with his custom in time-honoured film fashion was the look they were going for

I suppose and I hope it makes the final edit.

We've come to Cusco because tomorrow Paula, a female bear, will arrive and we have chartered a special train from Perurail to take the bear down, on a flat-bed container, to Aguas Calientes, at the foot of Machu Picchu, where she will be introduced to Yogi, the bear we rescued in the Paddington film, maybe for fun and frolics, but possibly with a view to a serious long-term relationship as they say in Lonely Hearts columns. Nick and Juan have to drive all through the night to sign a piece of paper to the effect that they have received one bear in good working order (and, of course, to hand over five hundred dollars): we luckier ones can sleep tonight and will meet them at a railway station an hour or so from here tomorrow lunchtime. We are advised to beg some umbrellas from the Monasterio as it has been raining for the past two weeks in Aguas Calientes, and when it rains in Aguas Calientes it really, really rains.

Sunday 3 February, 2002
Hotel Monasterio, Cusco

Last night Nick and Juan disappeared into the mountains with their $500. The idea was that they should return, with bear in a box, some time this morning. I came down to breakfast at seven thirty to learn that they were in the village all right, but that the box was the other side of a landslide. They couldn't exactly get her back to Cusco in the back of a van – bears need stout carrying cases.

This meant the rest of us, back in Cusco, had the day off which we took gently. Everything has to be done very slowly here. The lack of oxygen can affect some people very badly. I get a bit short of breath, but don't suffer the real headaches that afflict others.

Nick and Juan eventually turned up in the late afternoon – Nick looking like a raspberry lollipop. They had had one *bitch* of a day. The village where this bear had been kept (in a kind of squalid private zoo) was not in the least ready. Huge surprise there. Apparently the place had been decimated by Fujimori when he was fighting the *sendero luminoso* who had terrorised Peru for years and made it virtually a no go area for foreigners and indeed Peruvians. Fujimori defeated it (and Tupac Amaru, another terrorist organisation) by fighting fire with fire. The army had gone into every village where *sendero luminoso* members were even rumoured to be and, basically, taken no prisoners. The little city where the she-bear was awaiting us is rumoured to have lost up to ten thousand citizens who were suspected of s.l. affiliations or sympathies.

Anyway the result is The Most Gormless City in Peru: open sewers and a populace drifting around not knowing what to do. One of the poorest places in the country. When Nick arrived, and Nick Green it must be said, has all the energy, get-up-and-go, initiative and enterprise of an Empire Builder, he had to kick some serious arse to get the bear into the cage. First he had to build the cage. The one provided was basically a cereal packet to a bear. So for six hours in the beating sun he and Juan bolted and screwed and hammered and sawed until something passable existed. Darwin Mendivil, the marvellously level-headed and gentle vet we had met in the Paddington film, was there to help.

It was Juan's birthday too, what a way to spend a fortieth. But they're back now and tomorrow morning we will meet the bear on the train and film it en route to Aguas Calientes, film Mike Matson's computer webcam connections and see how the two bears get on.

'Yesterday was one of those
days. One of those good days.
One of those miraculous days'

16

Tuesday 5 February, 2002
Miraflores Park Hotel, Lima

The only time the air of Lima smells sweet is when you have returned from Cusco. Sea level oxygen-rich air, no matter how polluted with forty-year-old truck fumes, is a bouquet to be sucked down deep.

Yesterday was one of those days. One of those good days. One of those miraculous days. I have explained what poor old Juan and Nick went through yesterday in their attempt to make sure Paula was thoroughly paid-for, documented, checked for health and fitness to travel and furnished with a cage she wouldn't eat, claw or burrow through in seconds. Well, that means the day's tasks were:

1. To get up and go to a railway station outside Cusco where in theory two things would be waiting: a charted train comprising a carriage for us and a flat-bed travelling carriage for she-bear and a truck containing the bear in a cage.
2. To get caged bear onto flat-bed and travel to Aguas Calientes where Yogi, a four-year-old male has been living alone for eight months without ursine company of any kind.
3. To get Paula off the flat-bed and up a hill.

4. To see Mike Matson install his webcam into Yogi's enclosure, which has been separated into two sections.
5. To coax Paula into the empty section of Yogi's enclosure.
6. To film them meeting across the separating mesh.
7. To travel back to Cusco at a sane hour.

It's quite an ask, as they say in cricket. Knowing Peru, something would go wrong and something would require shouting, exhortation and the contents of Nick's pockets.

The first part went well. We got up and breakfasted at six-ish.

The second part went well. There was a train waiting. There was a bear in a truck.

It was also pouring with rain, the first rain we've had and the prospect of doing all our filming with John's camera wrapped in his high tech bin-liner (NB: Only use Sony approved bin-liners. We cannot otherwise guarantee the proper functioning of your camera) and myself under an umbrella was not appealing.

Still, we got the bear onto the flat-bed and were on our way.

Perurail is run, on behalf of Orient Express, by a wonderful Swiss called Yasmine Martin, who had arranged everything with fantastic efficiency. There were drinks and sandwiches on board for us and an exceptionally high quality selection of fruits for Paula. Paula needed to be tempted every now and again with grapes to stop her chewing at the wooden floor of her cage. One swipe of a paw and she had already got a plank jutting up which she was expertly prising out. She couldn't escape that way, but it would leave us the problem at Aguas Calientes of how to carry the cage up the hill without her falling out the bottom and heading for Machu Picchu above, which might have frightened the backpackers, which would never do.

Every now and again we stopped to let a scheduled train pass by. The local reaction to a bear gliding serenely past on the back of a train was something to behold.

Children ran to try and keep up. I imagine them being clouted around the head when they got home and reported what they had seen.

'How many times have I told you not to lie to me?'

'But, mum. I did! A real bear. On the back of the train. Eating grapes.'

'Right. That's it. Straight to bed with you until you learn not to make up silly stories.'

I remember a series in my childhood on the BBC called, I think, *Great Railway Journeys of the World* in which Paul Theroux or similar would cross India or Siberia on a train. I don't recall a Peruvian railway being filmed, Perurail didn't exist then of course, but there is no question that Cusco to Aguas Calientes is just about the most wonderful journey you can take on the planet. The gorges, peaks, and (at this time of year) the tumbling, spouting, splurging and quite terrifyingly fast and frisky Urubamba river have a surprise at every corner. I can do no better than quote Matthew Parris on Peruvian countryside, from his classic, *Inca-Kola*:

> *…a sense of something no English landscape can inspire. It is the feeling that what lies within vision is only just the beginning of what waits beyond.*

What waited beyond for us, of course, was the town of Aguas Calientes. If Machu Picchu is the crown on the top of Peru's head, it's a shame that just about the only way to get to it is by way of Peru's arsehole. For I'm afraid that's what Aguas Calientes is. It takes its name from the hot springs close by and is a shambolic collection of hideous buildings thrown up with no thought or consideration for the Eighth Wonder of the World above it. INRENA won't let the Machu Picchu Sanctuary Hotel fit a water purifier without a year-long wait for permits, but it will allow any citizen of AC to despoil one of the world's most wonderful places. (Polly, our stillsman Rob Fraser's partner, aptly calls INRENA the institute for national perks.) The citizens fight the plans for a cable car which would be one of the most sensational and beautiful experiences imaginable, because they fear for the monopoly they hold on bus-rides up the mountain. The whole place should be bull-dozed and a town of which Peru can be proud should be put in its place.

There are one or two remarkable people in Peru who work within the system to achieve great things. Jim Sherwood of Orient Express is lucky (or clever) enough to employ some of them, Yasmine of Perurail for example. Other great Peruvians we have encountered include Joe Koechlin who owns and runs the Incaterra (also known as Cuzco-Amazonia) Lodge where we stayed in Tambopata and who has built the only lovely thing in Aguas Calientes, a hotel called the Pueblo which includes an orchid walk and a wonderful use of two materials that reflect the great obsession of the Incas – stone and water. Joe made available for us at the Pueblo the land and manpower that enabled the building of Yogi's enclosure and he and his son Nacho (Ignacio) combine great business acumen with a fanatical devotion to the preservation of Peru's diverse habitats.

Another such is Roger Valencia, an ex-chemist who has gone into the tourism business and whose organisational skills were to prove very useful later in the day.

So, we've arrived in Aguas Calientes. *In bright sunshine.* It had been raining every day here for the last three weeks but for us it was clear and sunny and perfect. Maybe the

Gods of the Cloud Mountains had taken pity on Nick for the night they had put him through.

It was splendid to see Yogi again: in eight months he has been transformed from a forlorn, disease-ridden, mangy prisoner into a proud young bear close to full sexual maturity.

Mike Matson had been in Aguas Calientes for three days setting up his webcam and modem and power line, with the help of the puppy-like William Garcia who had been our Quechua (local Indian) interpreter and hilariously (in retrospect only) dangerous driver.

Anyway – step three in our to-do list as Americans like to call them was, if you remember, to get Paula off the flat-bed. First we had to remove a tarpaulin separating the two areas of the enclosure. For this Tim equipped me with his leatherman.

We had brought with us on the train journey the appropriately named Darwin, the vet who had helped us with Yogi last May. He felt that if we could do it quickly enough Paula needn't be tranquillised. This suited us: it's dispiriting to see a bear tranquillised and I've seen it more often than is usual in a lifetime. Apart from anything else the waking-up, bear-with-a-sore-head procedure would cut into our time enormously and we only had as much time as there was light.

Roger Valencia took charge here. The idea was that I should get involved, for the cameras, in lending a hand and holding one of the poles that made up her stately litter. Frankly when dozens of Peruvians start shouting and lifting things I have learned that the only sensible procedure is to stand clear.

It would never work. Her floor was loose. She was cross and confused. Although it was sunny, the steep, tangled hill the cage had to be taken up was muddy and slippery underfoot. The cage itself weighed half a ton and Paula is a big heavy bear who likes to careen backwards and forwards shifting the weight in a manner designed to disorient her porters. It would never work.

It did. In five minutes the cage had been taken up the hill, round the side of the cage and to the entrance of the Female Quarters.

The cage door was opened, she bounded into the enclosure and there it was. Done.

The big question now was: Would they like each other? Or even notice each other. These are two bears who have not been in contact with others of their species since they were born. Bears are very territorial, females as much as males. Darwin thought it was a fifty-fifty ball. They might roar and lunge at each other, they might be attracted. I wondered if it might not be a thirty-three, thirty-three, thirty-three ball. Perhaps they would just be indifferent.

What happened next melted every heart at the Pueblo. The strange mystery of how one species recognises another of its own is one thing: the mystery of love and

attraction has been the greatest theme of art and conversation since human beings stood upright. But it doesn't matter how often the story is told or the subject discussed. To see it with your own eyes is a privilege that every onlooker shares. Each pair of human eyes softened to tears and each human mouth stretched to the widest smile it was capable of. For forty Peruvians (and seven Englishmen) to be completely, stone silent is miracle enough. To hold your breath at that altitude makes you dizzy. We were all dizzy for the next half an hour.

In the male section Yogi was enjoying a watermelon.

In the female Paula lifted her nose to the air and leapt on top of a rock to press her nose against the partition. Darwin had told us that she was oestrous and fully ripe. Her nose told her that there was male bear in the offing.

Yogi continued with his watermelon, back to the female quarters, so we chirruped and coaxed him to a part of his section which offered a full view of the other side of the partition. He lumbered forwards, possibly expecting an avocado. Then he stopped full-gallop and twitched his nose.

They stared. They gulped. Yogi came forward. Their noses touched. Two tongues came out and they licked each other's muzzles. A kiss. Then — well, the pictures tell it best.

The first six steps had gone without a single hitch. I

did some breathless pieces-to-camera that I hope won't look too soppy and the train drew up to take us back to Cusco.

We left the bears desperate to find some way through the mesh that divides them. It felt cruel not to allow them together, but Darwin Knows Best. In two weeks' time, unless they have a row, the separating door will be open and, on live webcam we hope, their love will be sealed in more than a kiss. The prospect of cubs is too tantalising to think about.

We were back in Cusco by eight fifty. What a day. What a day. What a day.

We were up at five this morning to catch the seven-thirty flight to Lima. Tonight the Lima British Chamber of Commerce will host a dinner for us and I am to make a speech explaining what we've been up to. A ghastly prospect since I hate after-dinner speaking, but Nick thinks British interests in Peru can be very helpful to our Bear Foundation.

Tomorrow we fly back to London and the adventure will be over.

Epilogue

And so it ended. The news from Peru, as I write this in the midsummer following our return, is that Paula and Yogi are hopelessly, madly and impossibly in love. A pregnancy is extremely likely. The Bear Rescue Website – www.bear-rescue.tv – will keep you up to date.

Our intention is to use the money we have raised with this book and through sponsorship and other sources to purchase more land in Peru. This, in addition to the Hotel Pueblo land in Aguas Calientes that Joe Koechlin has donated, should enable the programme to develop further. Many people in Peru and in the United Kingdom have a knowledge of these bears that they never had before. Knowledge is the beginning of wisdom and wisdom the beginning of hope.

My thanks go out to everyone who has helped with this book, but principally to you, for buying it. Buy another copy to fill a friend's stocking and help a bear.

Acknowledgements

As the producer of both films — none of it would have been possible without the help of the following…

Joanna & Phillip Boyen
Sue & Ted Drinkwater — Screen & Music Travel
Claudia Cisneros
Rocío Barreto
Lucy Cardenas
William Garcia
Lima Zoo (Parque de las Leyendas)
Metropolitan Zoo of Santiago (CHILE)
Peru Rail
Orient Express Hotels and all their staff — Peru
Gabriela Lopez Guido - Aerojet
Joe Koechlin
Machu Picchu Pueblo Hotel
Inkaterra Lodge
Roger Valencia

BBC Television & Lorraine Heggessy for commissioning the programmes
Dip Sanghera
Jane Hewertson
Alliance Atlantis & Café Productions
Apple Computers
Mike Munn
Mike Matson
OR Media
Paddington Bear & Aunt Lucy
Michael Bond & Family
Stephen Durbridge and The Agency
Anthony Goff
Georgia Glover
Paul Gibbs
Andre Singer
Allegra Mcilroy
Sam Oakley and Harriet Green
Lucy Middelboe
Juan, Vangie, Alejandro, Maria Paula Tirado
Miranda Simmons
Julie Chang
Katherine Hall
Carrie Madu

Rob Fraser
Polly Sheesby
Alan Lewens
Tim White
John Warwick
Luisa Belaunde
Mr Valencia the taxi driver in Lima
Nick Green's Bank Manager
Lorraine Hamilton and Michael Symons
Roger Hart — British ambassador to Peru
The Embassy of Peru — London
The Ambassadors — Gilbert Chauny & Armando Lecaros
The Embassy of Peru - Chile
Pippa Isbell — Orient Express

And last but not least Stephen Fry

Thanks to you all — Nick Green.